The Gay Imagination

Alan L. Contreras

2024

Oregon Review Books

"The history of art doesn't suggest ... that great art gets made by aligning one's thought with everyone else's."

– Carl Phillips

ISBN 979-8-218-42673-6

Oregon Review Books
Eugene, Oregon

To the memory of

Joseph E. Evanich, Jr. (1960-1993), writer and artist

Lost in the deluge

Also by Alan L. Contreras

Nonfiction

Afield: Forty Years of Birding the American West
A History of Oregon Ornithology (editor with V. Thompson and N. Clements)
Antinous/David & Jonathan (editor)
Birds of Lane County, Oregon (editor)
Birds of Oregon: a General Reference (editor with D. B. Marshall and M. G. Hunter)
Collected Poems of Ada Hastings Hedges (editor with Ulrich Hardt)
College and State: Resources and Philosophies
Edge of Awe: Experiences of the Malheur-Steens Country (editor)
Handbook of Oregon Birds (with H. Herlyn)
The Mind on Edge: An Introduction to John Jay Chapman's Philosophy of Higher Education
Northwest Birds in Winter
Pursuit of Happiness: An Introduction to the Libertarian Ethos of C.E.S. Wood
State Authorization of Colleges and Universities (editor with R. Poulin, S. Thompson and C. Dowd)
TransPacific: Collected Poems of Ernest G. Moll (editor)

Poetry

In the Time of the Queen
Firewand
Night Crossing
Fieldwork (chapbook)

The Gay Imagination

Contents

Part 1: Writing

Part 2: Music

Part 3: A Conversation With Reginald Shepherd

Acknowledgments and Derivations

Many of the items in this collection first appeared in other venues. The list below indicates where they first appeared. Minor revisions have been made in some cases.

Front Cover: Bill Farrell's hand extended in front of an approaching storm, Diamond Craters, Oregon, photo courtesy Roger Taylor. The starry overlay from the Hubble space telescope is added to recall a late poem of Essex Hemphill, in which he, knowing of his coming death at age 38 from AIDS, expressed his own situation as departing into the constellations, where he would receive a new name. It also recognizes the speculative fiction of Samuel R. Delany.

The epigraph from Carl Phillips is from an interview in *Yale Review*, Spring, 2022.

Block prints by Eric Wuest are reprinted with permission from *Antinous/David & Jonathan* (Oregon Review Books, 2014).

Writing by Alan Contreras

"Alex Ross's *The Rest Is Noise*" appeared on *The Oregon Review* December 9, 2007.

"Andrew Marvell, Sexual Orientation and Seventeenth-Century Poetry" appeared in *Gay and Lesbian Review*, May-June 2018.

"Ashbery: The Songs We Know Best" appeared in *Gay and Lesbian Review*, Jan-Feb 2018.

"Black Phoenix" appeared in *Gay and Lesbian Review*, Jan-Feb 2019.

"The Bowerbird's Collection: Bebe Backhouse" is revised and expanded from a review that appeared in *Gay and Lesbian Review*, Mar-Apr 2024.

"Byron's Don Leon and Leon to Annabella" first appeared in *Gay and Lesbian Review*, Nov-Dec 2017.

"Carl Phillips releases *The Tether*" appeared in *Fireweed* 12:50, 2002.

"A Conversation with Reginald Shepherd" is abridged and adapted from *Song After All, the Letters of Reginald Shepherd and Alan Contreras*, issued as a fundraiser for the University of Oregon Creative Writing program.

"Deep Song: Federico Garcia Lorca" appeared in *Gay and Lesbian Review*, March-April 2021

"Essential Essays of Adrienne Rich" appeared in *Gay and Lesbian Review*, Mar-Apr 2019.

"A Glorious Wind: Ursula K. Le Guin's new translation of Gabriela Mistral" appeared in *Fireweed,* Fall 2003

"Honoring a Lost Poetic Voice" appeared in *Inside Higher Education* on October 16, 2008.

"Incurable: the Haunted Writings of Lionel Johnson, the Decadent Era's Dark Angel" is revised and expanded from a review that appeared in *Gay and Lesbian Review* May-June 2019.

"The Ins and Outs of Online Dating" appeared on *The Oregon Review* November 3, 2007.

"Isherwood in Transit" appeared in *Gay and Lesbian Review* Jan-Feb 2021.

"The Jewel-layered Tongue: The Journals of Samuel R. Delany" appeared in *Gay and Lesbian Review,* May-June 2017.

"Lovejets: Queer Male Poets on 200 Years of Walt Whitman" appeared in *Gay and Lesbian Review* Sep-Oct 2019.

"Ned Rorem and the Future of American Song" appeared on *The Oregon Review* July 28, 2007.

"Queer Natures, Queer Mythologies" appeared in *Gay and Lesbian Review* July-August 2020.

"Reginald Shepherd's *Orpheus in the Bronx*" appeared on *The Oregon Review* June 8, 2008.

"Richard Blanco's Lavender Conga" appeared in *Gay and Lesbian Review,* Mar-Apr 2024.

"Poetry of A.E. Hines" is revised and greatly expanded from a review that is scheduled to appear in *Gay and Lesbian Review,* Jul-Aug 2024. Special thanks to the poet for permission to quote the poem "Some Quiet Evenings" in its entirety.

"The Sacred Band: The Theban 300 in Love and War" appeared in *Gay and Lesbian Review,* September-October 2021.

"Unreachable Lorca" appeared in *Gay and Lesbian Review* January-February 2023.

E-mails and blog posts by Reginald Shepherd are reproduced here courtesy of Robert Philen, Shepherd's literary executor.

Writing by Reginald Shepherd (from his blog):

"Reflections on Poetry and Disaster" appeared July 2, 2007.

"Ann Lauterbach on Schools, Movements, and Poetic Identities" appeared July 8, 2007.

"Working Class Hero" appeared August 25, 2007.

"Gay Male Poetry Post Identity Politics, Part Two" appeared February 8, 2008.

Introduction

The question of whether there is a gay[1] esthetic is old and dodges a definitive answer, yet the "otherness" of gay people has consequences, and how that affects our creative work is a discussion unlikely to end. Fran Lebowitz asked:

> "What is culture without gay people? This is America, what is the culture? Not just New York. AIDS completely changed American culture... And with AIDS, a whole generation of gay men died practically all at once, within a couple of years. ... The first people who died of AIDS were artists. They were also the most interesting people... The knowing audience also died and no longer exists in a real way... There's a huge gap in what people know, and there's no context for it anymore."[2]

This view is that of gay people as culture-bearers as well as culture creators and interpreters.

There have been many interesting collections of essays and interviews on this topic, including Robert K. Martin's *The Homosexual Tradition in American Poetry* (1979) and Christopher Hennessy's *Outside the Lines* (2005), which has the advantage of letting a reader hear a number of gay poets discussing craft in their own words.[3] In addition, a number of gay poets have written their own essays on the art of poetry, which sometimes include material on gay life or gay themes.

The question of "writing gay" offered Edmund White a title for the first chapter of his essay collection *Arts and Letters* (2004), which includes chapters on many gay (and a few lesbian) writers and artists. The topic is also discussed in such books as Richard Canning's *Hear Us Out: Conversations with Gay Novelists* (2004). David Bergman has written a number of books about gay writers and how they fit into the American literary tradition, and also edited *Gay American Autobiography: Writings from Whitman to Sedaris* (2009), which lets a number of gay writers speak for themselves.

There are also books that offer a more specific subject or point of view, such as E. Lynn Harris's *Freedom in this Village: Twenty-Five Years of Black Gay Men's Writing, 1979 to the Present* (2009), which focuses on fiction but includes some poets. Other examples of selective work include letters, for example *The Animals: Love Letters between Christopher Isherwood and Don Bachardy* (2013), *Dearly Beloved Friends: Henry James's Letters to Younger Men* (2001) and Stephen Spender's *Letters to Christopher* [Isherwood] that appeared in 1980. Jonathan Alexander's *Writing & Desire: Queer Ways of Composing* (2023) provides a wandering, intensely personal and highly academic look at queerness in the world of creativity, both written and visual.

The poetry anthology *Queer Nature* (2022), edited by Michael Walsh, provides a good variety of work by gay poets whose eye and ear were tuned to the natural and outside world, despite J. D. McClatchy's admonition that nature is an uncongenial subject for poetry. These touch on themes of creativity and gay life from various angles and can provide some insight into how or if a "gay esthetic" is innate, develops or is applied.

There is no single universal gay opinion or point of view, nor is there only one gay esthetic or way of seeing. There are voices within the gay and lesbian community (as in other communities) who want to prohibit certain words or ideas from being seen or heard (see "The Danger of Uncontrolled Poetry" in this volume), but as Black gay poet Reginald Shepherd noted,

> "... a poem has never oppressed anyone, though I was once on a panel at a gay writers' conference with a black lesbian performance poet who implied that literacy was oppressive to black people, which certainly would have been news to the slave-owners who tried to keep their property from learning to read."[4]

Lesley Chamberlain, writing of Rainer Maria Rilke, noted that "[d]arkness is the poet's hour. Others should not invade it, with their gesturing and their chatter."[5] To some extent writing by gay people vis-à-vis the non-gay is like seeing a community at night rather than by day: the objects are the same, but the vision is not.

Whether we write of loneliness and love, travel, music, communities, rocks or tropical adventures, our reactions are often not quite what a straight person would have. We are *in* society but not *of* society, in the larger sense, and this will always be so, simply because societies solidify around what most people do, think and want. Most people are hetero.

As gay people, we can live and create more openly in some cultures than in others. The difference between being a gay creative in Indonesia, Norway or Hungary is not trivial. More locally, a community in Alaska will have different ways of doing things and thinking about things than a community in Alabama or Connecticut. Culture is real. We are not all the same in the social sense.

Imagination and Creativity

What do words like "imagination" and "creativity" actually mean? Imagination is a form of *creative awareness*, hearing a bell choir that many people cannot detect. This awareness can be situational, perceptual or take other forms. Creative people climb the same hills as everyone else, but having achieved the summit, they simply keep climbing because they can see steps not visible to others. This results in their work being generated from a viewpoint that only they can reach. It isn't necessarily a pretty process: Rilke once said "drive out my devils and I'll lose my angels too."[6] But the results are the great artistic creations that we know.

There are differences in a creative person's choice of subject, way of responding to it and choice of images in a response. Most writers want their work to outlast the perishable to achieve the eternal. An ideal created work gives value to those who engage with it not just this week, but indefinitely. Our best work should be varnished, not dissolved or petrified, by the caress of time. It should be continually perceived as worthy and esthetically valuable. Thus we still listen to Tchaikovsky, read Dickinson and gaze upon Caravaggio. This is the platinum standard: to live as nearly forever as humans can manage.

Should poetry always read like a spring breeze that has passed over a hundred open blossoms? No. It can be cold, harsh, brutal and of course boring. There are no forbidden subjects, words or forms. There are only questions of artistic effectiveness, which is largely a matter of the artist's intent combined with a given reader's reception. Over the life of a given work, each reader is different, as is each reading by the same reader. Some may react to a given work with indifference, others may cry, or run out the door bellowing with rage.

There are, or course, complex issues with poems written about or for specific political positions or historical happenings. Most don't age well simply because memory or salience of a given incident fades (see the chapter in this volume on the poetry of A.E. Hines for an example of a skilled poet avoiding this problem). A few, e.g. from the classics or more modern offerings such as Auden's "September 1, 1939," become more canonical. This is hard to predict: Auden did not like this poem yet it is among his best-known today, fifty years after his death.

Ellen Bryant Voight noted to gay poet Carl Phillips that poetry is not the transcription of experience but the transformation of it, which Phillips took to heart.[7] All creative writing is conversion to metaphor, a substitution of words for things and thoughts. The forms of fiction, poetry and drama are well-known and may approach the metaphors of life differently, but none of them *is* life, they are all representations using various mirrors, filters and conversions. Art and music have their own ways of representing.

What is "Good"?

A number of the essays in this volume began life as book reviews, though some have been greatly expanded from the original published version. As a reviewer, I need to share useful evaluative comments with the readers of my work. Just saying "I loved it" or "stinks bigtime" does not tell the reader anything that helps them decide whether to read the book in question. For this reason I tend to work backward as a reviewer after reading a book, first identifying a hypothetical audience for what is in the book. Sometimes this is obvious: a book marinated in footnotes and written in academic language can reasonably be flagged as directed to experts or researchers and less appropriate for high school students. Sometimes I need to use my experience to consider who the best audience really is. Thus my standard as a reviewer is essentially whether a book is fit for its stated or implied purpose.

That said, it is also possible to describe the way a given author writes in a way that gives a member of the appropriate audience an idea of what reading the book is like as a *literary experience*. A book intended as fiction, poetry or creative nonfiction should probably not read like a catalog or advertisement. Two books written for the same general audience may differ widely in style, thus they could be "dry as last month's baguette," or "written with casual humor and crisp wit," and so on.

There can also be questions of demonstrable substantive quality. These can relate to technical issues like typos, poor references, timeline failures, the way a work is laid out (do the chapters connect in a sensible way?) or such issues as factual inaccuracy regarding historical events, scientific knowledge or physical objects.

In addition, we may ask whether a given work is good in the sense of having added sufficient value to its field rather than being mainly derivative or a restatement of existing work. This rather misty evaluative category is less applicable in the creative arts than in other fields, yet is certainly applicable to, for example, biographies or other studies of creative people.

How do I determine whether my work, or the work of any other creative person, having worked very hard to make it, is "good?" Does the word even have meaning? Sometimes I have been a reader, proofer or reviewer for books or articles in my own fields (principally ornithology and higher education law), in which I am personally able to see errors of fact as they go by. More often, I am reviewing a book in a field in which I have a more general interest or some basic experience but am not an expert. In such cases my stink-o-meter is necessarily recalibrated and less active and my comments tend to be on more general aspects of the book. In this volume, most of the reviews are in this latter category.

Judgment and Experience

Poet and essayist Edward Rowland Sill wrote in a letter to philosopher Josiah Royce that "[y]ou never know in this world whether you were really casting pearls at all until you feel the tusks." Who judges quality? Are all who express an opinion about a work merely different varieties of swine?

Excellence in mechanics, public policy and government is at base dependent on the proper application of judgment to facts—the *facts* are the key pivot point—they simply need to be determined. We build bridges according to the physical norms of engineering: steel and copper have different properties, each absolutely necessary in its place. We make laws and regulations according to the functional requirements of constitutions and statutes. We build computers and aircraft according to the requirements of physics and electronics. In these cases, failure to follow the rules results in a mess, a disaster, a failure to work, a lack of social utility and so on. These things have to be done *right* or they are not what they say they are.

The imaginative arts are different. For the most part, instead of facts we rely on history, experience, custom and compiled opinion, which can collectively be thought of as *judgment* in the non-judicial sense of the term. In the arts, we each apply our own judgment to a work of imaginative art such as a poem, cantata or sculpture, and the key pivot points are many. At a minimum, the experience, breadth of understanding and knowledge base of the evaluator matter—there are no definitive facts in the same sense are there are in, say, the function of electricity, though there are often many pieces of information, some obvious, some less so.

Yet the market for creative arts may have a limited interest in quality even if we can identify it. This is nothing new and not really something to worry about. Dwight MacDonald, speaking in the 1950s of the emergence of a larger fiction market in the mid-1700s, noted "a new subjective approach in which the question was not how good the work is but how popular it will be."[8] More recently, Alex Ross, who specializes in classical music reviews (see the short book review herein), made clear that "[t]he trouble is, once you accept the proposition that popularity corresponds to value, the game is over for the performing arts."[9] Of course, some overlap exists between today's best-seller and work that lasts: we still read books that were written hundreds of years ago, and look at paintings of a similar age.

So what, exactly, is all this talk of quality, popularity and value about? The key issue is time. What work *lasts*? Yes, works do get rediscovered—Bach in his entirety, for one—and some works of great quality get lost, but in general, a work that still has an audience decades or centuries later has to be viewed as having value, whether we like it personally or not. Consider the poetry of John Ashbery discussed in this book. Whether we *like* it or not, its impact on poetry in general is undeniable (so far) and this is one thing that establishes value and quality.

Personal Taste and Cultural Development

Questions of *taste*, though, are ultimately individual, based on what we each know, with some of us having more knowledge of given creative arts and thus seeing a work differently. We don't have to care what is popular, we just have to care about what interests us. Ideally, in order to exercise evaluative thought about the creative arts, one must have a certain amount of exposure to them and, ideally, soak up the opinions of those with even more exposure.

Once we get beyond that point, a preference for Hockney over Warhol is ultimately personal. I personally prefer listening to Bach, Tchaikovsky, Brumby, Wilberg, Tallis, Scarlatti or Rachmaninoff and generally avoid Mozart, Haydn and, until recently, Gershwin. My tastes, weighted toward the Romantic and Baroque and skipping lightly across the Classical, have shifted over time as I gain more experience as a listener: Gershwin has moved from the Avoid column to the Why Not column. I have *learned* to appreciate and respect his musical writing. I'm making some progress with Mozart.

The same dynamic is true of poetry and fiction, though the choice of easily available writings is larger than for art and music. We all make our own decisions about what we prefer based on our experiences over time. These judgments collectively establish a cultural outlook on a given work of art or art form. Working within that larger culture are those people whose knowledge and experience allow them to understand and express more nuanced views of a given work, performance or idea. These are qualitative judgments; not everyone is prepared to make them, beyond liking X and not liking Y.

That's fine, but I think we benefit from paying attention to what the knowledgeable and experienced have to say. Mario Vargas Llosa points out that a culture including qualitative judgments has become hard to maintain because "the difference between price and value has disappeared...What is successful and sells is good, and what fails or does not reach the public is bad. The only value is commercial value."[10] Angus Kennedy wrote of this risk that

> ...the question of excellence starts to take a back seat to that of access and—by far the greater danger—the question of excellence begins to be answered precisely in terms of access....Or to use slightly different terms: the good becomes identified with what is fashionable and easy, while anything difficult and traditional is seen as bad.[11]

This is not new: Alaska poet laureate John Haines made a similar point in an essay in 1969—this trend is well-established now.

There is a fundamental question here related to the nature of the audience for excellence. In principle, anyone can identify, appreciate and understand excellent work. The point of limitation has mainly to do with an individual's understanding of the traditions and baselines of a given form of fine art or parallel professional norms, and our willingness to spend energy learning.

One key question is whether a given piece of writing, music or art is intended for a mass audience at all. This is what Kennedy calls the "utilitarian" view of art:

> ...the only way for the utilitarian to judge the value of a work of art is in terms of its impact on a mass of people: the more it impacts equating to how useful it is and, therefore, to how valuable it is. The end result of this approach ... is that we become indifferent to two things: to the work of art in itself and to you, the individual spectator.[12]

In the world of writing, Italian writer Cristina Campo expressed her concern about the nature of modern published poetry as follows.

> ...I've been leafing through a magazine bristling like a porcupine with impeccably momentary poems—one surpassing the next in its ferocious temporariness, scrambling feverishly to embrace the hour of its death—when a silence falls, the page opens like a pale, sea-colored sky, and a garland of verses settles on it, as pure as Ursa Major. Here is a poet." ... [if a poet fails to remain true to poetry], "Snatched up by the common maw, he is no longer capable of anything. He is *human* now. He is in *solidarity*. He is *consoling*. To put it plainly, he is no longer memorable. More than once we have seen such an albatross enter, out of politeness, into the cricket's cage.[13]

This view is, I think, congruent with that of Reginald Shepherd and Ann Lauterbach (see "A Conversation with Reginald Shepherd" in this volume). The question is not so much "what is poetry?," which is not amenable to a useful answer, but "why has this work been published?," a question that writers, publishers and readers need to think about. Just because I write something does not mean that I should publish it.

Particularly since the advent of very easy and attractive self-publishing, the slurry level has risen to the top of the flume and perhaps beyond, a mining-camp image that Auden might have liked. The sheer volume of published work limits what any reviewer, expert or not, can consider, and of course much of it is dreck. This very book that you are reading is in effect self-published. Whether it is dreck remains to be seen: you get to make that judgment based on your knowledge and experience.

Modern society is run according to the terms set forth by science and business. Yet science is a lava flow, only the front edge is still moving and doing things. The creative arts are a forest, alive no matter its age, a great web of connections that are still functioning. Likewise, business uses a set of evaluative tools that may not apply to music or poetry or fiction. We need to remain attentive to the need to apply useful, appropriate standards to things that are in different categories. Care must be taken to separate one's "day job" from one's creative work. Are we publishing because we must, we can or we should?

Always in the back of our minds should be the question: to what crude beasts are the creative arts yoked? We need to remain independent of the yoke, free to follow our ideas where we like.

What is in this book

The first half of this collection includes twenty-four of my essays and reviews, mostly focused on gay writers and musicians. Many of these first appeared in other venues, particularly *Gay and Lesbian Review*. Other original venues include *Inside Higher Education, Oregon Review* and *Fireweed*. Some appear here in print for the first time.

It may be worth noting that these writings do not claim to be in any way comprehensive or representative of creative gay and lesbian people. Most of them are about men, all of them are about writers (mostly poets) or musicians and many active, spectacular gay writers are not included. There is essentially no discussion of theater. The collection is thus idiosyncratic and represents a combination of material that has interested me over the years, as well as subjects chosen for me by journals for which I write reviews, principally *Gay and Lesbian Review*.

In addition, the first part of the book (divided between Writing and Music) includes several essays that relate more generally to the creative arts and have some connection to the gay and lesbian community. These are not reviews of any particular book or other example of the creative arts, but express some thoughts about creative processes and people that may be of interest.

The second half of the collection includes an extended conversation between me and the late Black gay poet Reginald Shepherd. This includes discussion of gay writers and how they relate to each other, including a transcription of an event conducted by Shepherd and Christopher Hennessy (growing out of Hennessy's book *Outside the Lines: Talking with Contemporary Gay Poets*) in which the question of "gay poetry" is discussed by a group of well-known gay poets. This section is adapted and condensed from *Song After All,* a publication I issued in 2013 as a fundraiser for the University of Oregon creative writing program.

Special thanks are due to editors Richard Schneider at *Gay and Lesbian Review* and Shelley Reece at *Fireweed* for allowing me significant freedom to write reviews for the magazines. Bill Farrell read and significantly improved the introductory material and aspects of the principal content.

Alan Contreras
Eugene, Oregon
April, 2024

The Gay Imagination

Part 1

Writing

Richard Blanco's Lavender Conga

(2024)

The Cuban-American writer Richard Blanco is a quintessentially modern poet, with promotional links throughout social networks and his own life as his primary subject. Add to this his gold-plated credentials as President Obama's inaugural poet and a National Humanities Medal from Joe Biden, and we have the perfect poster boy for modern poetry.

Homeland of My Body (2023) is a substantial compilation of poems from four earlier collections, along with many new poems. Blanco includes references to his private life in many of his works, but he does not write primarily about gay life. Instead, it is his Cuban ancestry and family members that shine through like a Havana sunrise. Ancestry, family history, and Cuban customs are so much at the heart of his œuvre that the theme of gay love is moved to the periphery.

That said, Blanco does sometimes write about love and relationships, and this more private side runs through the book like a lovely, shaded stream, slowly emerging from his Cuban roots. This excerpt from "Why I Needed To" contains a lot of gay Blanco in a small space: "because my husband, who's still scared of his adoration for me as we embrace sleep, still doubts how long I'll nest my dreams in his arms ... because I have never quite told him: *always* ... because I'm just as afraid of needing him more than myself." Note the casual domesticity of "my husband," the cuddly line "how long I'll nest my dreams in his arms," and the transitional exit line, the meaning of which is obscure and the tone a bit sappy. The poem goes on for many more stanzas.

Blanco has attracted a certain amount of criticism from traditionalists because of the way in which he combines highly personal subject matter and a tendency to edge into a maudlin tone, of which the previous quotation might be considered an example. Yet there are many poetic lenses that give us the three-dimensional language of art. Consider this passage from "Maine Yet Miami":

I rise
to the sun of my youth rising over the sea, after
a night's sleep on a bed of the sand, dreaming or
dreading who I'd become, or wouldn't. Though
I grew courageous enough to marry a man who
only loves me in English: *darling, sweetheart, honey*
I love him in my Spanish whispered in his ear
as he sleeps: *amorcito, tesoro, mi Cielo.*

Okay, this may be on the sentimental side, but it weaves a calm, strong web of family with the passage of time, the crossing threads of culture, and the inner feelings of a relationship. The pause at "or wouldn't" is particularly effective: we all have a self-image and life plan that is constantly being fine-tuned.

There are humorous moments in many of the poems: as when God, in the Beginning, creates Cuba rising above the waters and immediately starts tapping his foot to a conga. Much of the material about Cuba and his family flows along as a prose poem or simply a story, with poetic form not really a factor. However, there are plenty of poems that set forth Blanco's love for the island in tight, ringing word-chimes.

Sometimes his family history blends into a poem with a gay theme. The delightful, finger-wagging poem "Queer Theory: According to My Grandmother" is a long menu of things to avoid so you won't become, or be seen as, a gay kid. Thus: "Don't watch *Bewitched* or *I Dream Of Jeannie* / Don't stare at the *Six Million Dollar Man* ... I've seen you," and "Stop click-clacking your sandals, you're no Tropicana chorus girl." After two delightful pages of such admonitions, the poem ends with a warm-hearted "even though I know / you *are* one."

The emphasis on Cuba and family ties leaves ample room for reflections on love. A few lament the end of a relationship or its failure to quite achieve liftoff. One rather dark example sets forth a recurring dream of the death of his partner. Perhaps the most moving is "El Americano in the Mirror," which is structured (as are many of the poems) as a prose statement broken up into lines of poetry. The following is about young Richard's fifth-grade punching of another boy, and reads in part:

> Why didn't you punch me back? That would've hurt
> Less than the jab of your blue eyes dulled with pain—
> How you let your body wilt, lean into me, and we
> Walked arm in arm to the boys' room, washed off
> The blood and dirt. Is that how you remember it?
> What you can't remember is what I thought when
> Our gazes locked in the mirror and I wanted to say:
> *I'm sorry,* maybe *I love you*. Perhaps even kiss you.

It's worth the price of the book to read the entire poem, which is as good a description of young love as I've read. Blanco says here of his friend Derek what Gore Vidal, of an older and more reserved generation, never quite could about his teen flame Jimmy Trimble. There's a time and place for allowing emotion to shine forth from the sleeve, and this is it. Blanco casts a wide net as a writer, and the poems related to his love life are not the main course in this collection, but they offer an excellent selection of starters and sides.

"Taste is the expression of the pleasure a person takes in his own inner perplexities and satisfactions"
—J.D. McClatchy, from a Paris Review interview

Visions of Lorca

(2021, 2023)

Gore Vidal famously said that the three saddest words in English are Joyce Carol Oates. For gay readers three of the most iconic are Federico Garcia Lorca. Known to readers in English mainly by his maternal surname, Lorca occupies a tense junction in the histories of Spain, writing and gay culture. Dead over eighty years, he is as much a recurring comet as a poet or dramatist, barely fading before he reappears in yet another book, monument, musical fantasia or exhumation request. His gifts as a writer and the symbolic effect of his political murder aged 38 birthed a steady and remarkably varied artistic industry.

Lorca, actual or imagined, inspired many other artists. Poet Jaime Manrique entitled his 1995 collection "My Night With Federico Garcia Lorca," a night which Manrique imagined but did not have. Leonard Cohen named his daughter Lorca and is represented in an entire songbook based on Lorca's work. Other musical offerings include the song collection by Ana Belen, called, appropriately, Lorquiana—yes, Lorca was also a songwriter.

Lorca's Eternal Duende

Perhaps the most brilliant gem in the tiara of Lorquiana is the late Shane MacGowan's song for The Pogues, "Lorca's Novena." The lyrics begin with a blistering image of Lorca's friend the poet-matador Ignacio Sanchez Mejías gored and dying in the sand of the bullring while holding a single red rose (an image perfectly attuned to Lorca, though one of the books discussed herein notes that the matador died a few days later in a hospital). The sound begins as a distant dog howls under a dark, dense foreboding of guitars and ends with the rising tramp of military boots. The 'duende,' an infused spirit of genuine emotion important to Lorca, is as present in this music as Lorca could have wished.

Of published material about Lorca there is a wealth, with Ian Gibson's 1989 biography the anchor point to date. Gibson wrote several other books about Lorca, including one entirely about his assassination, an event that continues to fascinate the international public, despite the family's wish for a memorial park instead of another search for his corpse. Unique offerings on the Lorquiana tray include a selection of his letters, a long memoir of Federico by his brother Francisco and, perhaps of greatest interest to gay readers, Paul Binding's 1985 *Lorca: The Gay Imagination*, which focuses specifically on Lorca and homosexuality. In addition to inspiring writing about him, his work encouraged many poets and generated a speculative fire-dance of a novel about hypothetical immortal Lorcas, Carlos Rojas's *The Ingenious Gentleman and Poet Federico Garcia Lorca Ascends to Hell*. I'll stop there; the material is vast and kaleidoscopic.

The stage writing of handsome, doomed Federico offers social darkness lit by sparks of wit; his poetry whisks together previously immiscible images. This casting of visions upon the waters to see them interact in a reflective medium is part of what we think of as surrealism, but that was only part of Lorca, who was highly rooted in the details of ordinary Spanish life, as this well-researched book makes clear.

Comes now Stephen Roberts, professor of Spanish culture at the University of Nottingham, into this mirror-ceilinged performance hall.[14] It takes a certain confidence and clarity of intent to present a new biographical offering about such a well-known and vivid figure, with the faces of worthy predecessors gazing down like Lorca's floating face in Dali's paintings. For the reader whose interest in Lorca is basic, Gibson's biography will do. For those whose interest includes the details of how Lorca's writing came to be and how it is linked to daily life and culture where he lived, Roberts offers us a rewarding tour that, although sometimes apparently offering every possible detail, never gets tedious as it succeeds in walking the narrow path common to academic and popular writing.

Deep Song, a title borrowed from Lorca's own work, starts with Lorca's Garcia roots in the countryside of southern Spain, a blend zone with strong Arabic influences and a wash of unique culture that led to the poet's fame upon the publication of Gypsy Ballads in 1928. It is also a place of interconnected family and business relationships. Some of these were helpful to the young writer and some ultimately fatal, Roberts argues with evidence gathered from multiple sources and laid together like the mosaics of Andalusia.

In all of what he was and did, Lorca was a man of place. His poems overflow with the colors and smells of the rural land; his plays with the social and religious intensity of the old traditional homes and families in which he grew up, particularly with the thoughts and habits of the women of this society. His sense of disconnection when he lived in New York was palpable; less so during visits to Cuba and Argentina, but these places were still not quite his as was the countryside around Granada.

Roberts makes clear that Lorca was uniquely positioned in time and space to be the great flame of literature that he became, his genius gathering in aspects of rural and religious culture and in some cases filtering them through a remarkable array of creative friends and acquaintances. His intellectual guest list, many of whom were involved with his projects, included composer Manuel de Falla, painter Salvador Dali, philosopher José Ortega y Gasset, filmmaker Luis Buñuel and poet Jorge Guillén. Guillén noted that Lorca's lively and colorful personality was like an entire atmosphere and weather system.

We learn here that Lorca was liberal toward people and new ideas but a fundamentally conservative person in how he viewed life's roots. Strongly connected to rural agrarian culture and marinated in the deeply traditional Spanish Catholic Church, laden with saints and symbols, he lived and worked in the difficult junction between his sexual life and his fundamental culture. He was supported in college by his wealthy family but became something of a ne'er-do-quite-well-enough, eventually called to task to finish his formal education. This resulted in his getting a singularly inapposite degree in law, which was barely accomplished and may have left some sour feelings among his family's associates, some of whom could have assisted but did not when Lorca was arrested and killed.

The young Lorca, bullied as 'Federica' when a schoolboy owing to his effeminate ways, was by all accounts something of a slut once he achieved a comfort level about his desires, known for matter-of-factly asking for sex and indulging in it whenever he could.

He could not be called discreet: he was part of a traveling theater group in the 1930s that some critics called "Sodom on wheels."

Murdered in 1936 near Granada, the home town that had inspired so much of his best work, Lorca the martyr gained even greater fame that proved an irritant not only to the Franco regime but to Spanish authorities ever since. In MacGowan's song, one line reads "Lorca's corpse, as he had prophesied, just walked away." Some still seek his bones beneath the dusty stones of Spain; they dig in vain, for he is again risen.

Larger-than-Death Lorca

New articles and books about some aspect of the life and writing of Lorca appear often enough that a reader might be forgiven for thinking that no more can be said, or at least that no more need be said. That thought is complicated by the complexity of Lorca's life and work and the extraordinary expansion of interest in him since his death. Now we have *Lorca After Life* by Noel Valis.[15] Other books about Lorca focus on his poetry, plays and other creative work that happened during his life. The current volume succeeds in adding a useful layer to the great cake of Lorquiana by focusing less on the poet himself and more on what happens to cause a famous writer to become an icon.

The book's title is perhaps a necessary marketing hook upon which to hang this exceptionally detailed study, but half of the book is not directly about Lorca. It is about the artistic, political and social milieu of Spain and southern Europe in the first half of the Twentieth Century and what happened to the reputations of some of the major writers of this period. In addition to a discussion of the lives of such other gay artists as Pier Paolo Pasolini and Álvaro Retana, a chapter is devoted to what happens to the reputation of such creative artists after they are dead. Though the author has a rather ghoulish fascination with how many times certain famous bodies have been literally unearthed and moved, yet the idea of fame after death is important in a consideration of Lorca, as his transformation into an iconic immanence—a man never quite clearly seen or firmly grasped—began building shortly after his murder and continues to fascinate many today.

Valis notes that this not-quite-solid impression is augmented by "a multiplicity of Lorcas," as people look at the poet from a remarkable number of angles, poetic, political, social, sexual and more. Lorca's own innate shape-shifting complexities make the task of grasping a definitive Lorca impossible. We choose our approach to his misty Andalusian hilltop and get as close as we can to the immanent man.

This unreachability comes in part because "an air of incompleteness characterizes the man and his work" according to Valis. This is not the abandonment of given poetic works as French poet Paul Valéry would have it, but rather Lorca's constant creation of the new without feeling a need to complete the old. Efforts at closure of given aspects of his creative output were precluded in a technical sense by his early death, but he was always rushing forward spraying spectacular new ideas in all directions. As an artist, his fame was mostly in Spain until he went to New York and Latin America in his early 30s, at which time he was overwhelmed by an adoring public but had a short time to live.

Lorca's status as a gay man is treated thoroughly and from some unusual angles. The author asks what it means for Lorca to be a gay icon when he was not officially out during his lifetime and very little of his written work has something resembling a gay theme. Yes, the "Ode to Walt Whitman" includes some pointed language, not least the butterflies (*mariposas*) placed in Whitman's beard, as the Spanish word was a common term for gays. Likewise there are poems like the lament for macho bullfighter Ignacio Sánchez Mejías, memorable enough to inspire Shane McGowan decades later. Yet many gay men, some of whom were well-known Spanish poets, died during the Spanish Civil War, but Lorca's artistic reputation and status as a gay person now towers so far above the others that only experts such as Valis even know the other names. Why is this?

Some of it has to do with personality. Lorca, though perceived as somewhat feminine, did not like what he saw as flamboyance among gay friends or gay writers he knew of, such as the ultra-colorful trash-novel impresario Álvaro Retana, more famous than Lorca in the 1920s and definitely a *mariposa,* though not out. Lorca was, though artistically very advanced for his time, somewhat conservative in his personal manner and sense of connection to the old lands of Granadan and southern Spain. He had a mixed relationship with the idea of fame (veneration for his work) and celebrity (think Kardashianism), which are not the same thing. Gayness as a label was in its infancy and the fate of Oscar Wilde was remembered by people Lorca knew.

In theory, this old-fashioned social framework should have limited his visibility. Yet the great Spanish poet Jorge Guillén noted that sheer colorfulness was the essence of Lorca, who "was above all a wellspring, a fountain burst of radiance, the very clarity of the world's origins, freshly created and yet so ancient. In the presence of the poet—and not simply in his poetry—one breathed an aura illuminated by his own light."

Having read this scholarly investigation of how Lorca came to be the man and butterfly we see him as today, I can't help thinking of the young people who come to him as older generations did to Whitman. I hope that some extra gift of perseverance comes to the young gays who read Lorca's "Ode to Whitman," which, despite its strange ranting against flagrant public expressions of homosexuality, contains these lines:

> Wherefore my voice is not raised
> to admonish the boy who inscribes
> a girl's name on his pillow, Walt Whitman, old friend;
> not to shame the young man who dresses himself like a bride
> in the dark of the clothes-closet....

Lorca was not a modern gay man, yet he is a shining part of our cherished history. The Italian filmmaker Pasolini noted that it is only in death that the ultimate meaning of a life can be determined, as until that point the life is constantly changing and adding. Perhaps Lorca died at exactly the right time, when modern media were capable of promoting a charismatic and talented person, and under the right conditions, a murder with no corpse, to light the first flame of many that brought enough light to who he is—somehow he does not seem quite dead—and what he means to us today.

A Bowerbird's First Gathering: Poems of Bebe Backhouse

(2024)

Australian gay writer Bebe Backhouse comes to us most readily through *More Than These Bones,* his unique collection of poems and images issued in 2023.[16] The author, who is also active in Australia's broader entertainment world (see the half-hour interview on RedBox available via YouTube), is not yet well-known in the United States. Backhouse is a descendant of the Bardi Jawi aboriginal people of the Kimberleys region in northwestern Australia, and as such represents a creative voice not often heard in the gay community.

The first part of this substantial collection might, with apologies to Paul Simon, be called Fifty Ways to Love your Leaver, as it focuses, rather repetitively, on the ending of a relationship that seems, from the content of the poems, to have had quite a number of flaws, unclear expectations and misunderstandings by both parties. Despite the overextended theme, some of these poems have a special sparkle, and Backhouse makes effective use of last lines as a sort of rump-smacking wakeup for the reader, as in *pyrite*:

> don't get ahead of yourself and think for one minute
>   i want to be with you
>   i've been desperately longing for you
>
> i haven't spent the last decade
> dreaming of you
>
> you can't be the one who got away
> because
> i was the one who ran

Later portions of the collection contain poems that are more distinctive, for example this tense, lovely offering in both French (not shown) and English.

L'amour sans paroles

the words I wrote
have served their purpose
yet
it's the words I didn't write
that continue to haunt me

so
i wonder then
of the love you handed me
if you gave enough to serve your purpose
or are you haunted
by what you kept?

The latter part of the book also includes some moving poems about Backhouse losing his mother, including one about her call on his birthday that, having always come, did not.

Some of the poems stand out from the main theme of loss even though based within that theme, for example the shaft of life-affirming light we get from *blood moon*:

like the moon
we're allowed to eclipse too

and when we do
everything is okay
because the eclipse will never become darkness

the light always returns

it's the same
as the survival of the soul

This bowerbird's collection is also distinctive in that it contains not only poetry, but also drawings and photos that offer some extended context but are also free-standing art in themselves. There are other gay writers who have offered readers more than a single kind of creative work in a given collection. Lorca comes immediately to mind, as he tended to include small illustrations in his communications.

Of course, many writers tend to gather objects at least mentally. James Merrill certainly fell into this category as a poet of things noticed, especially if they were beautiful. John Ashbery not only noticed things, but picked them up, played with them and churned out dictionaries of material about them, beautiful or not. Pattiann Rogers layers all kinds of plants and animals into her poems, as does Michael Spring. Auden was something of a connoisseur of arcane mechanical equipment (mining drills and the like, pretty much guaranteed to not be beautiful) and Roethke reveled in images of raising plants.

J.D. McClatchy wrote that the difference between a novelist and a poet is that a novelist wants to flood while a poet wants to distill. This debut collection by a unique and potentially valuable voice is more flood than distillation, but one has a sense that much of the material had built up over many years and has finally burst forth, clearing the way for a new vision. With luck this new poetic talent will bring us some fine distillations in the future.

A.E. Hines: the Poetry of Perseverance (2024)

A.E. Hines's second collection *Adam in the Garden*[17] offers the essence of gay life in poems that range from intimate to nearly galactic. His points of view are remarkably varied, perhaps in part because he lives some of the time in North Carolina and some of the time in Colombia, the homeland of his husband. In addition, he lived in Oregon and soaked up some Northwestern experiences. This background supports a transcultural breadth of image similar to that of Richard Blanco, Elizabeth Bishop or Ernest G. Moll.

Yet these disparate habitats, with cardinals on one porch and motmots on another, plus a garnish of Lesser Goldfinches from Oregon, are more frames than sources, for the most part. This is because Hines is fundamentally focused on human lives, loves and social links, with place as a reference point rather than an anchor or principal subject as it might be for John Haines, Richard Hugo or Mary Oliver. In this, his work more resembles Bishop than it does Moll or Blanco. His poetic diction is both straightforward and lush, rich with both sensation and understanding, gathering the experiences of daily life and spinning them into garments reflective, inspiring and sturdy. The approach resembles McClatchy, perhaps, but is less high-church and less urban.

This collection, his second, has a smoothness, a natural flow of image and rhythm, that is a step up in terms of polish from his first collection. Along with poems about domesticity and friendship, he offers some tough-minded images. A poem about Matthew Shepard, "Postcard from the Dead," ends with this unexpected sweet shiver:

But for twenty years, for thirty, far longer
than I was alive, our people remember
my name. It blooms
from their lips like a cold prairie rose.

Only the best poets can write, as Hines does here, about a specific event in a way that can remain fresh and strong over time. Adding the word "cold" helps this line grip the reader like a cloaked (and icy) hand on the shoulder.

Another example of how Hines can make a single incident a near-anthem is the closing of his poem "The Night the Lights Went Out in Moore County, North Carolina," which is about the drag show that continued despite the local power station being shot up by a nutcase:

> ... know you'll find no wilting flowers here
> just at the edge of the stage. With its green
> stiffened spine, the boozy and voluptuous
> tulip takes no bows. With outstretched petals
> outlasting gravity and death, it refuses to bend.

This all-embracing floral metaphor for a somewhat political subject attached to a specific incident succeeds in getting around the problem that Merrill pointed out: the words beginning to stink as the tide of feeling goes out. These words will never stink despite the incident itself receding into history, because at their heart, the words are about us or people we know, and simultaneously about the core toughness of modern gay communities and individuals. Their meaning to gay people will never be exsanguinated because gay readers transfuse it anew as we read it.

As the examples above show, Hines is particularly effective with powerful endings. This is true in much of his work. There is also much tenderness, as shown in "Some Quiet Evenings," shown here in its entirety:

> **Some Quiet Evenings**
>
> I go out to sit with them—thin
> insects tuning their strings,
> the night's first bat casting
> in the breeze—and remember
> that evening, hot and windless,
> a new lover stripping

my bed, spreading my sheets
on the moonless grass.
Who were we then?
Young and swallowed
by the night. Unfinished.
Ill matched.
Sirius trudged across
my narrow field of sky,
the whole universe sliding
away, a little more life
slipping out of me, again
so briefly in love.
Some quiet evenings I go out
to sit with them, all the men
I've been, and beneath
that same quilt of stars retrace
my path, the weak orbit
of every man to touch me.

This delicate atomic swirl, as much watercolor as text, is as good a representation as I have ever read of the way many gay people, especially men, experience their extended sensual lives over time. The unique stew of momentary joys, what-ifs, men lost over the dark horizon of AIDS or simply in the churn of daily life is how most of us live. Line breaks like "a new lover stripping/my bed, changing my sheets" give the reader a spiced reorientation while adding a layer of tenderness. This poem by itself reveals many angles of Hines's warm, determined poetic voice.

His previous collection *Any Dumb Animal* is sometimes described as focused on the AIDS epidemic, but is in fact quite varied. Many of the poems are connected with his first long relationship and their adopted son, now an adult. Some of these are about the symbols and sequences leading to divorce, e.g. these lines from "Something Old, Something New":

Was I stupid to ignore how he cleaned out
his closet each season? Blind
to the department store boxes arriving

one after another, new blazers and jeans,
every old thing replaced by the new?

The poem "After You Left," containing many bird images, concludes:

I thought we were happy.
that we always would be. But ours
was the happiness of larks. At first,
diminished little by little
in the shrinking days. Here,
then gone with the autumn leaves

This first husband, whose left-behind objects had to be disposed of, once gave Hines a book as a gift, declaring the poet the gift he had given himself. The poem "Inscription" ends "Me, the book he never/learned to read."

The first collection also includes poems about Hines's relationship with his near-caricature of a knuckle-dragging, thoughtless father and ineffectual, tragic harridan of a mother, from whose hospital room Hines ultimately flees, "...saving the one person/I could possibly save ..."

Yes, the horror of the fatal AIDS years is here, perhaps most vividly expressed in the disco-floor fantasia "Bohemian Rhapsody, 1991" which might as well be called Suttee With Hunky Azrael, given the atmosphere of ecstatic self-immolation. Yet the general tone of the collection, somewhat more free-form and a bit less refined than *Adam in the Garden,* is not grim. One of the last poems in *Any Dumb Animal,* "From Our Train Window I'm Watching the Hills and Trees," concludes with quietly exultant confidence, including a slant salute to Leonard Cohen:

So afraid to be old, you say. Yet
like the crumbling buildings you admire,
that's how the light finally gets in
and the soul gets out—that, in the end,
you say, what makes them so beautiful.

Now, with this second collection, a step up in poetic maturity and as finely crafted as anyone could wish, Hines places himself with Mark Doty, Jericho Brown and not many others as a clear, necessary, strong voice among gay poets writing today. He proves that it is still possible to generate excellent poetry from happenings in our private lives. We can be thankful that Hines is still a relatively young writer and can offer us much more in the years ahead.

Shining Light from a Dark Time: Essex Hemphill at Sixty-six

(2024)

In today's socio-political climate, we often come across language suggesting that unwhite people have lacked either opportunity or success in a given field. Sometimes this is true, sometimes it is not. If we look at the picture of English-language poetry in the past seventy-five years, Black Americans have produced so much memorable work that they are, as a category, carrying the flag.

There are so many names worth noting that any listing can only be suggestive, but looking at my own shelves I see thirty collections by Black poets. Sure, half of these are by a few favorites, but the "longlist," if you will pardon the use of this cute modern marketing category, includes Lucille Clifton, Gwendolyn Brooks, Reginald Shepherd, Carl Phillips, Yusef Komunyakaa, Major Jackson, D.A. Powell, Jericho Brown and the poet discussed here, Essex Hemphill (1957-1995).

In addition, Samuel R. Delany is best noted as a writer of speculative fiction, but he was a poet, too. In addition, my shelves contain a glorious memoir by the young Black writer Darnell Moore and, looking a bit outside our limited American box, a spectacular collation of images by the Aboriginal Australian poet Bebe Backhouse-Oliver.

Of these, many are gay. We never hear of a shortage of gay poets, but gay poets are no more likely to live, think or write the same way as as any other category of gay people: our sexuality is a beautiful but somewhat random gift. We do not expect the same kind of poetry from Hemphill and Brown, or from either of them and Daryl Hine.

Hemphill once went out dancing with Black gay poet Reginald Shepherd, but they had little in common as writers. Hemphill was a lightning-flame activist for both Black and gay causes, with cocks, holes and n-words an everyday thing in his writing.

Shepherd was a word-stirring classicist, not particularly at home in the world of modern share-all poetics.

In looking at the broad universe of Black gay poets, who is Essex Hemphill and why should we insist on keeping his light alive as his ghostly sixty-sixth birthday passes? In short, he was one of our best fire-carriers. For a thoroughly researched look at how Hemphill fit into the social and political environment during the epidemic years of AIDS, see *Hold Tight Gently*, Martin Duberman's book about the work of Hemphill and Michael Callen.[18]

I will not try to duplicate any of the immensely inspiring work that Duberman put into his book, but rather will offer a few thoughts about how Hemphill fits into the sizable array of gay poetic voices. That said, it is worth noting that Duberman, who rightly considers Hemphill "an undersung poet of major importance in Black cultural circles," includes extracts from a number of Hemphill's poems (some from an unpublished corpus called *Domestic Life*) that are not otherwise easily available because they were not included in his iconic, and now rare, collection *Ceremonies*.[19]

If I were asked which out-of-print American poet I'd like to see back on the list of available work, Hemphill would be on the short list.[20] His essays are of value, too, in part for their historical utility, but also, in some, for what they show us about families and love and keeping things inside. In *Ceremonies*, there is a short essay in which Hemphill explains the emotional stresses of giving his loving but presumably unaware grandmother a copy of one of his collections. She turns out to be more aware than he expects, with a completely different angle on his situation: "Do the authorities know what you are writing?" This turns out to be a cause of laughter and bonding instead of sadness and separation. Her use of the weighty word "authorities" is something of a period piece, though today's political climate suggests that we remain alert lest such ways of thinking become more prevalent.

Hemphill had little patience with anyone, black or white or anything else, who objectified black men. He made clear his objections to Robert Mapplethorpe's images of naked black bodies that in Hemphill's view were essentially zoo animals, devoid of faces or heads. Edmund White defended Mapplethorpe on artistic grounds, and Hemphill found himself arguing with Black editors who did not want him to line up on the same side of the issue as then-Senator Jesse Helms, a notorious right-wing bigot.

Hemphill wrote a number of poems in which his concerns about government involvement in sexuality were featured. One of these, clear and uncomplicated, is "The Occupied Territories":

You are not to touch yourself
in any way
or be familiar with ecstasy.
You are not to touch
anyone of your own sex
or outside of your race
then talk about it,
photograph it, write it down
in explicit details, or paint it
red, orange, blue, or dance
in honor of its power, dance
for its beauty, dance
because it's yours.

You are not to touch other flesh
without a police permit.
You have no privacy—
the State wants to seize your bed
and sleep with you.
The State wants to control
your sexuality, your birth rate,
your passion.
The message is clear:
your penis, your vagina,
your testicles, your womb,
your anus, your orgasm,
these belong to the State
You are not to touch yourself
or be familiar with ecstasy.
The erogenous zones
are not demilitarized.

Hemphill did not have a large output, partly because of his early death at 38. His essays were probably as well-known as his poetry, especially after he became known by way of televised events. Yet the poetry remains some of the most intensely celebratory we have from that or any period, and simultaneously among the most outspoken. Duberman reprints all or part of many of these, including this from "Vital Signs," when Hemphill knew that his time was limited.

> ...come stir
> The ink blue dusk with me,
> Come stir it with me
> 'til it's thick enough
> To rub onto our skins,
> Massage into our thirsty pores and follicles,
> So that distant stars
> Might see themselves
> Reflected in our shiny
> New blackness,
> And the planets, too,
> And the galaxies where our new names await us
> In full bloom, their succulence,
> The taste of victory will dribble
> down the sides of our mouths,
> sweet juice that will cause us
> to be high with liberation
> when we announce our new names.

It is hard to imagine a more uplifting elegy to one's own existence, with its celebratory rising awaiting the great change that comes to us all. The "galaxies where our new names await us" is an extraordinary and spectacular view of our time of passing and change: timeless love becomes a new constellation.

Samuel R. Delany: the Jewel-layered Tongue

(2017)

The first volume of journals from the great writer of speculative fiction Samuel R. Delany was published in early 2017.[21] For those of us who grew up reading Delany's science fiction novels and who have benefitted from his exceptionally detailed books on the craft of writing, there are so many mouth-watering bits in this first twelve years of journals that it is hard to know what angle of approach to take in order to catch just the right shimmer of light.

For those less familiar with Delany's career, it may be useful to mention that he was born in 1942 and these journals begin when he was fifteen years old. This is not obvious from the quality of the writing, which could be that of a graduate student in literature. At sixteen this appears in the Journal:

> I must stop being so analytical when I read; and be more so when I write. I have lost more effect from the greatest works of literature than anybody in the world—I bet. That's it! I'm too chemical. I know too much about what is being done with the words and themes. Although I can whip the words into place myself, I can see the scars on the backs of the words whipped by other writers.

By the time he was well into high school his erudition was absurdly advanced, as was his reading list. Yet what stands out even at that age is the absence of fear in how he writes and his choice of subject. One can apply excellent technique to a deadening array of daily banalities; Delany lived and wrote even then as if he saw extraordinary visions that most people did not. Sometimes this is reflected in his journals, for example in a loose series of vivid descriptions of fantasized casual sex on subway cars, in farm-boy trucks and backwoods porches.

There are also little asides that spice up the flow of ideas and plot summaries: "They say that Homer was a blind man led by a young boy. I don't know about you, but when I was a young boy,

I was warned to stay away from strange old men." Or this little gem:

> For poetry I say to the unwary
> Is passion with a dash of dictionary

It didn't take long for Delany to decide that he wasn't a young boy anymore—he was vigorously and variably sexual by his late teens and has stayed that way ever since, a walking, humping exemplar of the true breadth of human sexuality freed from irrational social constrictions.

One of the unusual aspects of these journals is that here and there we read the words of his then-wife, the poet Marilyn Hacker, whose comments are often a perfect combination of perception and snark:

> I know a young man called Delany
> Whose verse isn't overly brainy
>   When you start to get with him
>   He completely drops the concept of rhythm
> And eventually doesn't bother rhyming, either
> Which would be all right if
> He didn't start out
> With it.

This is but one of many delightful little interludes that pop up from Hacker, one of our best living poets. She and Delany were married for several years and have a daughter, but were always rather free-floating in their sexuality; today Hacker identifies as lesbian and Delany as gay.

Mixed in with a wide variety of plot ideas and miniature stories are aphorisms that stand out both from the page and for their content, e.g.

> Since Lord Byron, most art has been constructed so that the audience identifies with the myth of the artist rather than the body of the artist's work.

That may be more true of Delany himself today, as he has become an icon—the Black gay ambulatory monument of the urban literary universe—than it was in his early years. It is easy today to forget just how astonishingly creative and productive those early years were. Delany published—not just wrote, but published—*nine* science-fiction novels by age 26 (five by 23), including *Babel-17* and *The Einstein Intersection,* both of which won the Nebula award as best novel of the year from the Science Fiction Writers of America. One fascinating aspect of the journals is that they contain all manner of early scene-setting, character ideas and other speculative planning for these and other stories.

There are also delicious carvings made from people he knew in New York in his youth, such as this sly commentary on W. H. Auden and his partner, the more promiscuous Chester Kallman:

> "Where are you going," said Wystan to Chester
> "The boys in the park are a very bad lot
> The sore on your cock is beginning to fester
> And what can they give you—that I haven't got."
>
> Critic do not beat your breast
> Though Chester Kallman is a pest
> And must have done strange things to broaden
> The attitudes of Wystan Auden.

Well, that pretty much gets it out there.

Delany had a clear understanding of the genres he worked in from the beginning. At 23 he wrote:

> . . .
> SF is the literature that posits man is changing.
> Mainstream is the literature that posits he cannot change.
>
> Science fiction is the only heroic fiction left today; it's the only fiction today that admits there is a solution to its problems.

> Mainstream fiction is like looking in a mirror. SF is like looking through a door.

One interesting aspect of the journals is that Delany's science fiction plots, characters and ideas are remarkably varied and constantly fresh, while his sexual fantasy vignettes are, if not the same story repeated, certainly variations on one basic theme: young black man meets rough blue-collar white cracker and sucks him, often with one or both parties peeing, too. The difference between the mind and the body in action?

In any event, these journals are well worth a dive. We can indulge ourselves in Volume 1 and, while waiting for Volume 2, return with pleasure to *Dhalgren*, *The Jewel-hinged Jaw* or even, if you didn't get enough pig sex, *Hogg*. Seldom such an active body, seldom such a facile mind. Enjoy.

The Theban 300 in Love and War

(2021)

"It should here be noted that the military aspect of Greek love ... was nowhere more distinguished than at Thebes." – John Addington Symonds (1873)

Albert Camus once wrote that "if, to outgrow nihilism, one must return to Christianity, one may well follow the impulse and outgrow Christianity in Hellenism." It's hard to imagine a better introduction to at least one historically important time in the Hellenic world, and one with obvious contrasts with Christianity, than the fifty years or so in which James Romm takes us on a geographic, social, religious and military tour in *The Sacred Band*.[22] The book carries the subtitle *Three Hundred Theban Lovers Fighting to Save Greek Freedom*; in fact the Theban lovers were out to stomp the enemies of Thebes, there being no Greek nation-state at the time, but the hyperbole is ok—if you can keep track of who the enemies were on a given date.

The book is a tourist's guide to death in war, various kinds of suicide and sacrifice, the nature of gods and what they (might) want and a dizzying spin of alliances that come and go and back again so fast that you'd think they had the Internet. The period covered is stated as 378-338 B.C. and the location today's Greece, but in fact the time period covered includes explanatory material and connective tissue from somewhat earlier times in a region from Sicily to Persia.

The eponymous Band of the title is a select cadre of heavily armed infantry made up of male couples, typically one older than the other but all adults. The underlying theory (largely from Plato) of why this group existed as an effective formation in Thebes is that soldiers fighting alongside their loved one are, by definition, fighting for more than the government, and also that a male soldier would not want to show any whiff of cowardice or a failure of masculine discipline in front of the male soldier whose lover he is, owing to the nature of the male psyche.

Romm notes that the use of an erotically charged regiment "posed a distinctively Theban answer to Spartan values: instead of machtpolitik and the cult of the state, the Band relied on a native tradition, the view of male eros as a long-lasting, privileged bond." Same-sex relations were common and not a social issue in Thebes and in at least one other city, Elis. By contrast, the cult of Sparta, championed by Xenophon, was one of physical purity and sexual denial. Even playing around with women was scorned, let alone enjoying other men.

Romm is persuasive that this theory of "The 300" is at least plausible and probably the most likely explanation of the unit's establishment, actions and unique burial after its final battle. This last fight, which ended with the destruction of Thebes, was nominally against Philip of Macedon, but in fact the 300 were up against Philip's son, the eighteen-year-old Alexander, not yet Great (his father was murdered two years later) but an exceptional tactician who recognized that the Sacred Band was the heart of the Theban army both in terms of effectiveness and symbolic morale value.

For a reader interested in the social and military history of Greece at that time, the book will no doubt be of interest from the first pages, as the author is unusually gifted in offering a narrative that is readable by a non-specialist while hauling a remarkable number of names, relationships and alliances along the trail. I sometimes felt carried along, but never lost. For those whose interest is more specifically in the evidence about what the 300 were, what they did and how their possible manly connections were perceived at the time and by scholars since, you need to get 100 pages in before the bulk of this material appears. Yet as the story unfolds, the research supporting the idea that the 300 were in fact a gay male regiment is presented clearly, so the journey is worth the price.

Sources for the story include Plutarch, Plato (generally pro-gay), Xenophon (generally anti-gay) and others. Plato's *Republic*, written about this time, includes reference to a warrior caste that would also be trained in higher values. Given that Plato, in the *Symposium*, also includes a specific reference to an elite corps of male lovers, the connection with the Band seems quite likely. The contemporaneous tales include some nuggets: Xenophon, who disliked Thebes, noted that the Spartan King Agesilaus once made a stupid political decision because his son was in love with the son of an opponent. We also get to meet Sostratus the Fingertipper; you'll have to read the book to fully appreciate his specialty.

Is the book mostly about these gay warriors? No. Is there a lot of detail about how these men actually lived? No. Is the paired-male thesis sufficiently central that it works as a core to the narrative? Yes, though Romm can get a little breezy in checking off evidence and making connections, perhaps because as a professor who specializes in the classical period he has much of the history by heart. If we sometimes get a larger dose of regional history than is strictly necessary to advance the main theme, there is little sense of wasted language or too much time trotting on a particular hobby-horse.

Getting back to nihilism, although this period in history was not anti-gay in the sense we'd use the idea today—in some ways the opposite in parts of Greece—it was certainly a time of extremely rough problem-solving, with people leaping or being thrown from cliffs, routine destruction of entire communities, and related gore and indifference to what we would think of today as human life: Zeus giveth and Zeus taketh away, it is what it is, get over it.

For the most part, these folks were not using their words, though in a couple of cases a really good oration had immediate effect. What makes this relevant to our interest in a homosexual military unit is that little in the record suggests that these fighters were ill-treated or even considered strange (outside of Sparta) because they were what we would call gay. Occasional disparagement crops up in the limited historical record—one man's mother objected to him running off with an older man, shades of *Maurice*—but so does professional encomium.

The idea of a gay male military unit, probably based on this example, is still used in fiction today: Kate Elliott has a cavalry unit made up of self-exiled gay men in her *Jaran* science-fiction series. Romm notes that the Band was most fully understood by Plutarch among classical writers, and may have been an inspiration for Whitman's Calamus No. 34, the original manuscript version of which reads:

I dream'd in a dream of a city where all men were like
  brothers,
O I saw them tenderly love each other—I often saw them,
  in numbers, walking hand in hand,
I dream'd that was the city of robust friends—Nothing was
  greater there than manly love—it led the rest,
It was seen every hour in the actions of the men of that city,
  and in all their looks and words.

This is as good an image of the Sacred Band of Thebes as we are likely to find. Fortunately we now have a worthy reference to their times and their glory.

Whitman's Fruit-bearing Forest

(2019)

This year marks the 200th anniversary of Walt Whitman's birth, though the poet seems to be reborn on an irregular basis for various derivative purposes. Thus when I received the small book titled *Lovejets: Queer Male Poets on 200 years of Walt Whitman,*[23] I sighed and assumed it would be the kind of insipid, self-congratulatory, gayish poetry that we sometimes see in casual collections from little-known publishers.

I have never been more wrong about a book. This collection is one of the finest anthologies of poetry that I've ever read. The fact that all of the poems are either by or about gay men and their experience speaks to the power of our creative community. This collection has been assembled into a perfect pocket volume whose spectacular editorial content is matched by a well-crafted physical product. For all its portability, there are almost 290 pages of poems here, laid out in a distinctive, readable font on good paper in a solid binding. Editor Raymond Luczak has done the heavy lifting and brought us a pocket book of gay male poetry—he calls it a hymnal—that I for one will return to again and again.

One of the most exhilarating aspects of this collection is the way it gathers and honors the varied voices of gay male poetry from many years of writing. We read, for example, Jericho Brown, one of our best living poets, writing to and about Gerard Manley Hopkins, Essex Hemphill, and A. E. Housman, a poetic embrace of Whitmanian breadth. In "After Essex Hemphill," Brown writes: "Somebody ahead/of me seeded the fruit-/bearing forest." This lusciously entwined recognition of our gay poetic forebears in a few tight lines exemplifies what much of this book is about.

These poems often connect one gay poet to another in a lovely and poignant way. The late Reginald Shepherd is memorialized by Timothy Liu and Roberto Santiago. The latter re-uses the title "You, Therefore" from one of the best poems in Shepherd's 2007 collection *Fata Morgana* for a new poem that is wonderfully reminiscent of Shepherd's own merger of line-flow and word-banging.

Then there are such delights as Alex Gildzen's celebration of the body à la Whitman part by part, including such gems as "Brad Pitt's Thighs," "Jude Law's Lips," and so on. Fortunately the dubious idea known as a "prose poem" is rarely brought in, though it works well in the case of Trebor Healey's "A Nightclub South of Market" about Allen Ginsberg, part of which reads:

> "Ah, dear father, graybeard, lonely old courage-teacher, clown and boy of song, what America do you leave behind and which do you look forward into? What reincarnated infant are you now, a baby of Dharma, born with its heart outside its body, struggling to breathe and longing to love."

This is a clear Ginsberg image, yet much of it is Whitman, too. Healey also reminds us, in a pæan to Cavafy and his taste for young men off the street, that "Gods are not like wine/they don't age well."

In one of the more direct inter-poet references, Charlie Bondhus channels James Merrill in "The Science of Séance," a colorful takeoff on Merrill's Ouija-board gossip in *The Changing Light at Sandover*. Notwithstanding the line "I vant to suck your teat" complete with bogus Transylvanian accent, the idea and execution are quite entertaining. We also read intentionally Whitmanesque pieces, such as Gary Boelhower replicating Whitman going down to the waters naked. Then there are some delightful fantasias on Whitman, like the sweetly modern and typically self-promoting Whitman of M. J. Arcangelini, who brings us "Walt Whitman Poses for *Bear* Magazine."

Some of the poems are reprinted from other sources, sometimes from other decades, and some seem to be written specifically for this collection. This eclecticism could have been clunky; instead, it gives the collection a timeless feeling that's enhanced by the theme of poems written to or about other gay poets. Some modern poets are strangely absent, such as Mark Doty, Carl Phillips, the late J. D. McClatchy (who is, however, memorialized by Liu). It may be that reprint rights could not be obtained. But there are certainly enough poems here to last us a while in a collection of voices that contains multitudes, like Whitman himself.

Isherwood and Mishima

(2021)

Among gay writers who emerged from the first half of the Twentieth Century, Christopher Isherwood remains one of the most studied. One reason for this is that large amounts of material about him are available, with the bulk of his private papers held at the Huntington Library in California, largely from a donation by his long-time partner, artist Don Bachardy. A new collection of essays called *Isherwood in Transit* [24] grew out of the latest round of research; it is based on papers presented by seventeen writers at a conference at the Huntington in 2015.

In many cases repackaged conference presentations make dreadful books, readable only by specialists with magnifying glasses, and of interest only to them. Happily, Isherwood in Transit is much better than many collections and contains a number of chapters that will be of general interest not only to gay readers but to those interested in the particular milieus through which Isherwood wandered, in particular Germany and Japan.

These wanderings are the focus of the volume, whose editors have produced previous books on other aspects of Isherwood's life. The idea of "transit" is here taken rather broadly, with both physical travels and what might be called internal transits, e.g. Isherwood's religious experiences. Even Isherwood's entirely fantastical Mortmere stories, compiled with Edward Upward during their college years, are covered here. Isherwood once said "Perhaps I had traveled too much, left my heart in too many places," but it is this peripatetic habit that gave us much of his best writing, as this volume shows.

The Mortmere material, like the Vedanta chapters, are essentially a specialist's trove, though Mortmere gives an idea of Isherwood's early willingness to write more or less publicly about things normally considered private. He is not unique among gay writers in wearing his heart on his sleeve, but unlike most he placed all his private selves on display and labeled each so readers could not mistake what they saw. He famously began *Goodbye to*

Berlin with the phrase "I am a camera," but in fact that camera faced both ways, a sort of image-gathering disco ball that recorded whatever it saw and eventually wrote it down, using some material several times.

Unlike, say, Gore Vidal, Isherwood was quite comfortable with the idea of himself as a gay *person*, not just someone who happened to like sex with men. This general comfort level was loosely constrained by the cultural norms of the mid-Twentieth Century, but he still pursued his interests in a very matter-of-fact way. This includes his relationship with a young German that was pried apart by international regulations in 1938: Heinz was conscripted into the German army as WW2 began.

The most broadly interesting of the chapters are those on his time in Germany, his transition into California life, the background and writing for *A Single Man* and, most of all, the fascinating and detailed chapter called "Pacific Rimming," which covers Isherwood's visits to Japan in 1938 (briefly) and a longer visit with Don Bachardy in 1957. This latter event is chronicled mostly in a journal that chapter author Jaime Harker, a professor at the University of Mississippi, has sifted for nuggets.

What emerges in "Pacific Rimming," anchor point for the book, is a capsule study of the nature of Japanese sexuality shortly after WW2, with extensive discussion of what forms sex tourism took in that period. The fact that Isherwood disapproved of the mechanical nature of much of this activity make his observations all the more poignant, as in this journal entry on the "sex-colonists" he knew:

> "...[he] boasted suggestively of his conquests in bathhouses ... Ah, how disgusting this sexual colonialism is! And how guilty of it I have been, myself, when young! On the one hand, there is a quite vehement cult of the Japanese; it is regarded as tasteless and almost perverse if you dream of any non-Japanese sex partner. And yet, how these people despise the Japanese in their sex-relations with them."

Thus the 53-year-old journal-keeper links his visit to Japan after WW2 to his youthful pursuit of young German men in Berlin during the difficult interwar years in Berlin, when sex was easy for a visiting Englishman to get.

In Japan, this was not limited to gay sex: Harker calls the open available femininity of Japanese women compared to stuffy European women "a kind of wet dream for heterosexual European men" who had stumbled into a garden of sexual possibilities perceived by Americans as acceptable in Japan at the time.

In that same year, Isherwood met Japanese writer Yukio Mishima (pen name of Kimitake Hiraoka), who visited Los Angeles on a book tour. Mishima, who had been a popular companion at age 20 for American servicemen at the end of the war, had developed a taste for American men and, according to writer Faubion Bowers, once "flew over to America just for sex."

Whatever his other activities may have been, Harker sets forth the developing friendship Mishima had with Isherwood (and his own lust for Bachardy). Isherwood assisted Mishima with gay community contacts in Los Angeles and San Francisco during visits, but also with professional connections, e.g. referring Mishima to publisher Frank Taylor, who helped the visiting Japanese with U.S. publication of a short story collection.

Mishima was more or less "out" after publication of *Confessions of a Mask* in 1949 in Japan and 1958 in the U.S. This book involved the narrator's apparently intertwined desire for homosexual love and death. Mishima's magnetic attraction to young men combined with his fame as a writer allowed him to eventually drift into cult-leader status, leading to his creating a small private army, issuing a challenge to a Japanese military unit and almost immediately killing himself and having his head chopped off by a disciple.

Not long before his colorful departure (chronicled in the 1985 movie "Mishima: A Life in Four Chapters" with a score by Philip Glass) he wrote to Isherwood with the unexpected news of his marriage to a woman. The 1958 letter, discussed in some detail in "Pacific Rimming," includes this plaintive, hopeful and doubting passage:

> "... I could not get any perfect happiness from my long gay-life and now hope to get it (or its elaborate counterfeit) with my heterosexual marriage. Strangely it seems to me that I might get it with not so much difficulty. Do you think it is my wishful thinking?"

Two years later he was dead at age 45, leaving two children; Isherwood wrote in his diary "I suppose he had become completely crazy. I just cannot relate this to the Mishima we met." These sections about Japan and about the way Isherwood viewed Mishima and the nature of male leadership are exceptionally well-thought-out and presented. Anyone with an interest in Isherwood or in Japanese culture and sexual patterns will find the book a worthy acquisition.

John Ashbery the Hunter-Gatherer

(2018, 2023)

When John Ashbery died at 90 in September, 2017, some lamented the passing of America's greatest living poet. No one agrees on what is meant by great — I prefer Merwin — yet I was in a restaurant refreshing myself for this review by reading Ashbery's early work when my server stopped at the table and said "Oh! I love Ashbery. Especially "The Trees." That she, a random twenty-something, knew and liked Ashbery's work from sixty years ago seems to add at least one fresh brick to the pedestal whose accrued layers have steadily lifted him above the scribbling swarm as a poet of lasting impact.

There is surely broad agreement that Ashbery was our most *influential* living poet. His style was so distinctive that, as Alfred Corn noted in the November-December 2017 *Gay and Lesbian Review,* "we'd never heard anything like it." We still haven't. Whether that is good or bad is for poetry readers to say. I find some of his poetry immensely moving yet some does not convey meaning to me at all. Ashbery's poems certainly have a lot *in* them, but what can be gotten out of them? This has to do, as always, with the reader.

If Ashbery's writing did not exactly lead to a school, it certainly generated an argumentative classroom of poetry. His way of writing was a breath of energy to many poets of the last half of the 20th Century. Having felt his infused word-spray puffing into their ears, some ran to their desks, pen in hand, while others fled gibbering into the shrubbery. They all still do these same things, which speaks to the breadth of his influence.

Songs of the Fruit Packer

Now comes *The Songs We Know Best: John Ashbery's Early Life* by Karin Roffman.[25] The author, whose knowledge of poetry is considerable, chose to spend a lot of pages on Ashbery's childhood and its influences. For some biographies this energy would be misplaced. Not so with Ashbery, whose childhood experiences and images remained a recurrent part of his core work for his entire life. Roffman wisely spent time on these origins, including the poet's childhood and school years. Looking back to some of the juvenilia included in this book, two things come to mind. First, the work of teenage Ashbery, hiding his sexuality in diaries and coded Latin phrases, is remarkably similar in style to what the mature writer gave us. The Ashbery 'sound' was simply enriched over time; a stew perpetually renewed with new ingredients added to the same pot. Also, his juvenilia were shockingly advanced, much like Delany's, not only in how he used words, but in what words he used. This was a teen who was reading Hazlitt under the bedsheets.

His photographic memory apparently allowed him to retain every word he saw, and he deployed this varied collection of terms at seventeen with a clarity that must have been blinding to his contemporaries (and his teachers). A parallel among 20th Century creative artists may be Benjamin Britten simultaneously digesting Mahler, Berg and Beethoven in his teens at the same time as writing and hearing his own distinctive work performed.

We are then treated to his early years in college, hearing himself called 'gay' for the first time while cruising the bars. During this period he was still sending smokescreen letters to friends, pretending to be interested in women and trying to seem straight at Harvard, which at the time expelled known homosexuals. He managed to remain in college while ramping up his sexual exploring, returning to his family farm and its hated apple-packing chores as needed.

Although Ashbery is best known as a poet, he also wrote plays and fiction. One of the hilarious moments in his college career was the 'premiere' of the parody *Return of the Screw*, which involved "a Harvard student's nearly erotic encounter with a Dean Flotcher." Later serious plays included *Everyman* and *The Heroes;* the latter was produced to good reviews. He also performed in work by his friends and was given such delicious lines as "reading my diary I recaptured our old depression," from James Schuyler's recently rediscovered short film *Presenting Jane*. The film was based on activity of their friend the artist Jane Freilicher and also starred the poet

Frank O'Hara. Ashbery could also be appallingly direct with friends and colleagues: imagine saying to the young Samuel Barber "but I don't think you *should* write another major work."

J. D. McClatchy wrote in *Twenty Questions* that "The bowerbird in me is forever collecting colored threads and mirror shards to make a sort of world." He has nothing on Ashbery, who had a delight and facility in the placement of found objects into his poetic output. Other writers do this to some extent. James Merrill incorporated high-culture bric-a-brac, Auden used arcane industrial objects, Pattiann Rogers the names of all kinds of wildlife. Modern song-writer Stephan "Sparkbird" Nance (see this volume) masterfully displays his colorful collections of bird names and images from daily life.

Most writers of the purple page have a destination in mind that is at least broadly visible to the reader. Ashbery, though, sometimes baked word-cakes with unusual ingredients but gave the reader no real idea why crêpes made with pineapple and opium found a place next to formaldehyde, tulips, farts and swans (today's contest: which objects are from a single Ashbery poem and which did I invent?). That he was once inspired to write a poem simply to have fun listing the contents of thesaurus entries is therefore not a surprise. One of his high school couplets carried a foreshadowing of many works yet to come:

So, musing, she fell asleep, still sorry about the bed
Glad of the flickering stars, now green, now red.

Whoever criticizes this poem adversely must admit that it is at least bizarre.

Yet there is a lyrical, boy-in-love Ashbery who is sometimes missed by those who lose their way in his glittering word-storm. The poet asked in his own words: "Is there something intrinsically satisfying about not having the object of one's wishes, about having miscalculated?" Roffman notes that he recognized in his childhood what he rediscovered at Harvard: "unrequited love was good for his writing." His memory for words extended in the emotional arena to long-term recollections of specific experiences such as ill treatment at Deerfield School, obscure happenings in his family and boys he had wanted, the latter a growing and rapidly-changing list.

Ashbery was to a certain extent a reactive poet. Throughout these early years we see how his dry periods, some of them lasting many months, were often followed by significant flurries of poetic creation apparently originating from an incident, work of art, person met or another writer's work. One of the great strengths of this book is that the author understands the nature of the creative process and offers clear descriptions of how some of the inspirational sequences happened. Yes, she is using some of Ashbery's own diaries, which helps, but a biographer still needs a sense of judgment to sort out what is worth mentioning and what is not.

Roffman gets a little headlong when she plunges with a slight air of desperation through Ashbery's slut period in his late 20s shortly before he left for France. She makes a valiant effort to accurately track and describe in short sentences who was simultaneously sleeping with whom, angry with whom and working with whom among his large collection of friends and artistic colleagues. I'm not sure the result, though entertaining, was worth the effort to include in the poet's history.

In general, the last section of the book feels the weakest, perhaps because it is so clearly a transition. This is true not only because these young people were starting to swim into life's diverging channels but because Ashbery became a 'known' poet with the selection of *Some Trees* for the Yale Younger Poets prize and almost simultaneously left the continent. We can feel his story's oxygen being sucked to Europe several pages before the poet is.

I have never mentioned a book's cover in a review but this time I must. The leafy photo of a tender, teenish Ashbery picking cherries in the family orchards was taken by his father Chet, an accomplished photographer as well as farmer. Its use as the entire cover, with a superimposed "postcard home" bearing the title, is a choice of genius, presumably by jacket designer Sarahmay Wilkinson. The photo has meaningful links to every chapter of the book and is a poignant, perfect image of the pleasure and pain of formative youth, which were immensely significant to Ashbery's writing.

The publisher took a design risk with this unusual cover and got a gold medal result. How many book covers make you cry?

I hope that the next chapter in this glorious life is written, if not by Roffman, then by someone whose mastery of detail and story rises to her standard. It is a high one worthy of its subject.

Ashbery in Context

Ashbery is described by Jess Cotton in her compact biography[26] as "at once notorious and celebrated" owing to the perceived difficulty of his work. This short but thorough explication of Ashbery's life and work does a fine job of placing him both as a Twentieth Century poet and as a leading figure among gay writers. The book is part of a series published in Great Britain that includes scores of biographies focused on the writer's work, including well-known gay writers such as Jean Genet, Allen Ginsberg, Yukio Mishima, Marcel Proust, Susan Sontag and Tennessee Williams.

Ashbery came of age as a writer during the 1950s and 60s, a time in which gay people, though beginning to push back, were still smothered under McCarthyite social oppressions. Cotton notes that this may have been a factor in Ashbery's tendency to use language that was layered with hints and tinted representations rather than waving his flowering sexuality in the open. In this he paralleled his gay contemporary James Merrill, who, somewhat like Ashbery, is known as a poet of ornate surfaces rather than the kind of intensely intimate sharing that has characterized much of English poetry in the past forty years or so. As the author notes, "[for] a young queer child growing up in a traditional all-American family, evasiveness was a means of survival."

Cotton notes that after a semi-out period at Harvard, Ashbery became more relaxed about his sexuality during time spent in France in the late 1950s. During this period his style began to take the hunter-gatherer shape that it would retain, featuring all manner of bits and images of life that he felt made a true image of culture and daily existence. Ashbery rarely met an object, name or idea that he could not fit into a poem. Unlike Hart Crane, whose style sometimes looks similar but whose ornate waterfalls are mostly fancy words, Ashbery's glitter-froth tends to be from physical objects and, unlike James Merrill's refined displays, feels more discovered than constructed. The result became an opus of shimmering images rushing at, into and past the reader—the Ashbery style. He was not the only poetic collector in his era, as Ginsberg, Burroughs and Corso were exploring a kind of found poetics as well, and Robert Duncan's partner Jess was a collagist in the traditional sense, but Ashbery became the lighthouse for this approach.

Yet he was not just a poetic bowerbird gathering colorful objects for display. No one could say that lines such as "I'll brush your bangs/a little, you'll lean against my hip for comfort" lack lyrical beauty or are in any way obscure or picked out of a random word-pile. He was a prolific writer on art as well as about poetry. Sometimes his other writings attracted comparative attention, as when Mary McCarthy grumped that she wished his poetry were as clear as his prose.

Unlike poets who require uninterrupted solitary time, Ashbery was a profoundly social creature, welcoming and enjoying people and building various interruptions into the flow of his poems. His poetry is un-linear to begin with, often a series of observations, switchbacks, bubbles, oxbows and bursts, much like life itself, which he celebrated and which became the Ashbery style, at least the most frequent and visible one.

By the 1970s, Ashbery was more comfortable riding the wave of visible gayness, living with his long-time partner David Kermani and talking openly, if playfully, about Gay Pride, which he apparently felt, but without a need to be public. Like Merrill, Ashbery was not a noisy presence in the gay rights movement of the 1970s and 80s. He tended his private poetic gardens, gave Harvard lectures on poetic subjects and focused on his many friendships and on-again, off-again writing projects. In his longest poem, *Flow Chart*, written during the AIDS crisis and published in 1991, he assigns himself a role of one invisible gay person among many:

> It occurs to me in my home on the beach
> sometimes that others must have experiences identical to mine
> and are also unable to speak of them, that if we cared
> enough to go into each other's psyche and explore

> around, some of the canned white entrepreneurial brain food
> could be reproduced in time to save the legions
> of the disposed...

Not long after this, Ashbery's work to that time was the subject of a book by John Shoptaw, *On The Outside Looking Out,* which discussed Ashbery's work in terms of its "homotextual" content, which Ashbery considered unduly reductive. He grumbled about being treated as a gay symbol, e.g. for New York City's John Ashbery Day and as an official national icon for LGBT History Month in 2011. Cotton notes that he objected to 'the notion that gay writers are sort of expected to talk about sex or their sex lives in public.' Ashbery was too private a person for this and rarely alluded to gayness in a specific way in his poetry. He expressed to an interviewer that "I don't write about my life the way the confessional poets do," noting that his life generates experiences that in turn are the basis for poems.

The late gay poet J.D. McClatchy once wrote that the "20th Century's characteristic innovations [are] collage and abstraction." If that is true, surely John Ashbery's place as one of the main anchors of this movement is secure. That he was a well-known gay icon, whether or not he enjoyed being such, is a source of pride in the larger community of gay people of which he clearly enjoyed being a part.

Sam See's Queer Vision Quest

(2020)

Sam See was a professor of English at Yale who died in 2013 at age 34. For those interested in the strange details of his short life, involving his husband, escort services, court orders, and miscellaneous strife, the news media has all those. See's specialty was queer issues and themes from the classics through the early 20th century. The collection[27] discussed here contains previously published and complete but unpublished material, with an introduction and three essays by other writers. It is essentially a Festschrift focused on the main themes of See's work. The book is long, dense, academic in nature, and thus largely of interest to specialists in the field. If you are comfortable navigating a text featuring words like anacoluthon, chiasmus and catachresis, this book is your natural habitat, deep in the outgassing bayous of critical technical English.

Nature is one of its major themes, with a long chapter on rooting ideas of queerness in the works of Charles Darwin. This chapter is frustrating, as it trawls Darwin's writings for examples of uncertainty and the inherent unpredictability of the natural world, using those as hooks on which to hang an overly broad speculation that queerness as a cultural fact exists as a consequence or an inevitable parallel of constant variability in nature. At one level this seems too obvious; at another it seems a theory too far, grasping for inchoate possibilities. After all, humans are as much a part of nature as are squid, and the constant flow of DNA and natural selection affects all of life. Likewise culture is in significant part based on what nature allows: we eat fish and build with wood, not the other way around.

The question of what queer really means is a constant in this collection. Sometimes See seems to use the term to mean homo- or at least not mainstream heterosexual; at other times queer seems to mean anything that isn't in a majority or part of a received tradition. This fuzziness around a key term causes some of the essays, especially the one on Darwin, to feel slippery: the fish may be there but we never quite catch it.

A curious lack of understanding of science—perhaps simply a dismissal—bubbles throughout See's work. Academia usually values the fact-finding role of science, yet Heather Love notes in her superb closing essay that "See's writing on myth is linked to his writing on nature by a willingness to credit feeling as both evidence and justification: ... to foreground feeling in this way—at the expense of truth—is to break with the norms of academic discourse." This tracks with Eve Kosofsky Sedgwick's view, revisited by Love, that living within a personal myth that brings happiness is superior to knowing the truth.

This is all very well so long as the person cocooned within their own preferred cotton candy has no expectation that anyone else will join them in this tinted habitat or, for most purposes, recognize that it exists. Unfortunately, what is currently labeled as interpersonal respect and validation causes a certain social gravitation, a philosophical drain-circling through which people who might otherwise be truth-oriented become immured in the sticky outer webs of the myth-dweller's fantasia.

There are, to be sure, some real gems in this collection. The segment on Langston Hughes and how his work has drawn up Havelock Ellis as from a hidden spring, is much clearer than the Darwin segment and, though still requiring serious attention to detail, the leaps and connections that See makes are easier to follow. This is a real contribution to our understanding.

This is also true in the discussion of Hart Crane's *The Bridge*, in which See does not attempt to find queerness under random rocks but leads the reader to the lovely segment in which Crane closes by gently clasping Whitman's hand. Eliot's *The Waste Land* also lends itself to a fairly straightforward commentary owing to the presence of Tiresias, that mythical character with snake issues and an alternating set of sex organs.

Whitman has his own chapter, more or less, in which his interactions with Wilde are discussed. See concludes that

> "Whitman seems to have had no use for Wilde's aesthetic practices, even as Wilde had use for Whitman's: Indeed, Wilde admired that Whitman 'carries nature always in his heart' and claimed that Whitman was 'the simplest, most

natural and strongest character that I have ever met in my life.'"

One difficulty in any kind of poetic exegesis is that what can be read into a poem changes based on changes in the reader's knowledge base and æsthetic sensibility. It is impossible to state in most cases that what the poet "meant" can only be one thing. The very nature of poetry suggests the possibility of multiple meanings. This necessity of accepting and even celebrating ever expanding meanings is particularly necessary with writers such as Whitman, Crane, Eliot, and Pound, and See's deep knowledge of all of them provides for a lush if sometimes strained tour of poetic possibility. I wish he had lived long enough to give us a guided adventure in Merrill's *The Changing Light at Sandover*. That would have been a book by itself.

There are discussions of beauty and art here, including Wilde's concern that art should not raise nature on high (reminiscent of J. D. McClatchy's view that nature was an uncongenial subject for poetry, suitable only as a backdrop for human issues). One of the best is a revisit to Crane's "The Bridge," in which the phrase "Appalachian Spring" appears, the source for the title of Copland's ballet score (courtesy of Martha Graham). In the poem, it is not a season but a source of pure mountainside water, one for which we constantly strive. Sam See burned bright and fast like Crane; those who study queer imagery and myth-making will be glad to have this compilation.

Adrienne Rich on Life and Culture

(2019)

Adrienne Rich was a 20th-century poet who wrote essays and criticism with the same ease, effectiveness and insight that she brought to her major craft. This ability places her in the company of Reginald Shepherd, Carl Phillips, James Baldwin and a relatively small cohort of others. Rich, like Baldwin and Gore Vidal, was exceptionally engaged with social issues of the day. These writers—along with Ursula K. Le Guin and a few other so-called "public intellectuals"—were in effect successors to Lionel Trilling and others of the early 20th Century. This new generation appeared on schedule; what changed was their subject matter. The Cold War and its precursors and baggage were no longer the controlling influences for writers who began their major work from the late 1960s onward.

Rich was one of the great bridge figures in this generational transition. A critic of how capitalism functioned in daily life, particularly its impact on women, she was not particularly interested in the rhetoric of socialism or its history. She was interested in how society worked for real people right now, rather like Gabriela Mistral or William Stafford, and that preoccupation appears throughout this volume, edited by Sandra Gilbert.[28] It can be seen in an extract from her famous essay, included in the collection, called "Compulsory Heterosexuality and Lesbian Existence":

> The New Right's messages to women have been, precisely, that we are the emotional and sexual property of men, and that the autonomy and equality of women threaten family, religion and state. The institutions by which women have traditionally been controlled—patriarchal motherhood, economic exploitation, the nuclear family, compulsory heterosexuality—are being strengthened by legislation, religious fiat, media imagery, and efforts at censorship.

Little in this 1980 essay seems out of place in the American political and social environment of 2024.

Rich excoriated what she saw as a "retreat into sameness": an assimilationism that she regarded as "a renewed open season on difference." The idea of difference came to her slowly as her life progressed from her days at Radcliffe through heterosexual marriage and widowhood, and to an eventual and extraordinarily fecund lesbian awakening. Her poetry collection *A Change of World* won the 1951 Yale Younger Poets prize. W. H. Auden, the judge for the prize, notoriously said that her poems were "neatly and modestly dressed, speak quietly but do not mumble, respect their elders but are not cowed by them, and do not tell fibs." Notwithstanding the patronizing tone, this was a rare critical misunderstanding by Auden, who seems to have missed something powerful in Rich's work that other critics have acclaimed.

This collection (*Essential Essays: Culture, Politics and the Art of Poetry,* Sandra Gilbert, ed.) is large enough to include all of "Compulsory Heterosexuality" and also a long chapter about Emily Dickinson called "Vesuvius at Home." This includes an extensive, perceptive analysis of the poet and her work. It also sets forth certain little-known facts, for example, that some of Dickinson's poems about or to people existed in two forms, one with male and one with female pronouns. This is the detail-oriented, scholarly Rich who is so effective at supporting an argument.

More than many of her contemporaries, Rich recognized the role of the poet as teller of unpleasant truths to society, and she saw poetry as a tool to accomplish this task. Unlike a poet such as Merrill or McClatchy, whose poetic focus was on the happenings of their own lives, arranged on a glass shelf slightly above the messy churning of society, Rich was all about writing to produce change. She pointed to the many forms of male power as it is exerted over women, everything from economic oppression and physical abuse to genital mutilation and denial of education.

Rich found significant differences between lesbians and gay men, including divergent economic opportunities, very different approaches to sexuality, and a pronounced ageism among gay men. She was a lifelong critic of capitalism and specifically its impact on the arts, and worried that "an apparently disengaged poetics may also speak a political language—of self-enclosed complacency, passivity, opportunism, false neutrality."

A theme that runs throughout this collection is her dissatisfaction with feminists who don't want to acknowledge the importance, or even the existence, of the lesbian experience in society. She notes that "feminist research and theory that contribute to lesbian invisibility or marginality are actually working against the liberation and empowerment of women as a group." She considers lesbian existence to be a form of ordinary life and dislikes the term "lesbianism" as sounding clinical. Rather than an "ism," it is simply an aspect of being female that many women experience—one does not develop a lesbosis for which one sees a doctor.

Rich declined President Clinton's offer of the National Medal for the Arts in 1997, stating in her letter to the president that

> "art ... means nothing if it simply decorates the dinner table of power that holds it hostage. The radical disparities of wealth and power in America are widening at a devastating rate. A president cannot meaningfully honor certain token artists while the people at large are so dishonored."

Among Rich's heroes was Walt Whitman, whose wide-open vision of what America could be struck her as "vistas of possibility, not odes to empire." That open horizon of possibility is what she wanted all women to have in their own right, not as adjuncts to men or even in opposition to men but without reference to the position of men. It is a sharply critical but ultimately positive vision for all of us.

The Glorious Wind of Gabriela Mistral

(2003)

The Chilean Nobel Prize-winning poet Gabriela Mistral spent much of her life in a domestic relationship with Doris Dana, a relationship viewed today as fundamentally lesbian. Her writing was not about relationships in the way that her former student Pablo Neruda's was. Mistral wrote more about society, about people's lives, about the dailyness of things.

Whenever a writer as powerful as Mistral is translated by a writer as distinctive as the late Ursula K. Le Guin, the result is likely to be unfortunate or glorious.[29] Le Guin taught herself Spanish, though she doesn't speak or write the language, but poetic translation requires as much esthetic sense as linguistic facility. She also issued her own translation of Lao Tzu (she does not read Chinese, either), and has now brought forth not only the largest collection of Mistral's work ever available in English, but a translation of great beauty, filled with the sensitivity to subtleties of human experience that we have come to expect in her own novels and poems.

Any translation is the creative work of at least two people. The key to a successful translation is to convey as much of the original writer's meaning as possible without the translator's own creative personality burning through. There are four previous substantial selections of Mistral's work in English: a 1957 selection by Langston Hughes, a sizable block published in 1961 by Mistral's domestic partner and literary executor Doris Dana, Maria Giachetti's 1993 "Reader" that also includes some prose, and Christiane Kyle's large-format illustrated edition of *The Mothers' Poems* issued by Eastern Washington University Press in 1996. The latter has relatively few poems but is visually spectacular.

These four have significant differences in selection and none is complete. Neither is Le Guin's; with her characteristic directness she simply says that she was unable to translate some of the poems satisfactorily, so didn't. Nonetheless, this is the largest collection now available in English.

How should a translator approach a poem? With respect, modesty and trepidation, one hopes. Yet excessive caution can drain the life out of a poem and convert it from inspirational art to a technician's wordpile. We can be thankful that Le Guin knows how to balance respect with boldness, thereby filling the English words with the same earthy fire for which Mistral is known in Spanish. Consider how she handled "The Foreigner," a poem that appears in all three of the previous major collections. Le Guin's version in its entirety reads as follows:

"She chatters about her barbaric seas,
seaweeds and shores that nobody here knows.
She prays to a bodiless weightless god.
She looks so old she might die any moment.
She's made our own garden alien to us,
planting cactus and saw-toothed grasses.
She breathes life from the desert wind,
and she has loved with a blanching passion
that she doesn't talk about, and if she did
it would be like the map of another planet.
She'll live among us eighty years
always as if she'd just arrived,
speaking her panting, whimpering tongue
that nobody can understand but animals.
And here among us, on some night
of fearful agony, with only her fate
for a pillow, she'll die
a silent death, a foreign death."

The word "seaweeds" is a good example of Le Guin's esthetic sense leading her to the right poetic word, not just the right English word. The Spanish in this line is "algas," which is a general word for algal plants. In theory the Spanish for seaweed should be "algas marinas," yet in the context of the lines, "marinas" is clearly not necessary because the first two lines are all about seas and shores, thus "seaweeds and shores" is both accurate and poetically superior in English to what two of the other translators used: Giachetti's "mystic algae and sands" (a strange combination in English:

mystic algae?) and Dana's "sands and algae unknown to me." Hughes also had the good sense to use "seaweed," though his line "God knows what seaweeds and God knows what sands" seems overcooked, since the "God knows" parts are not in the Spanish at all.

The very first line gives an idea of what poets do in translation. The poem begins "Habla con dejo... ." which translated literally, means "speaks in a slight accent" (Hughes version) or perhaps more precisely, speaks with an odd accent. Le Guin starts simply "She chatters," which does not convey the meaning of "dejo" very accurately, yet in the context of the poem as a whole, fits very well, because this foreign woman is babbling away about all these strange things, and "chatters" also suggests that the sounds are less than understandable, much as an exotic parrot or monkey might sound.

Compare this to the technically purer but boring Hughes version or the Giachetti version "She speaks with abandonment" and Dana's phantasmic excursion: "She speaks with the moisture of her barbarous seas still on her tongue," far afield from the words of the original but poetically the most vivid. Le Guin has stopped at the edge of the revisionist abyss, Hughes never got close to it, Giachetti is off on an uninspiring side trail and Dana has leapt the abyss in one stride, in effect presenting her own images filtered through the original. Such is translation.

Le Guin does not always choose the word I would choose—for example, her "saw-toothed grasses" is milder than the "claw-like" grasses of Hughes or the dangerously active "clawing grasses" of Dana, which I like best because it fits with the idea of a strange, foreign, uncomfortable, possibly dangerous garden. Giachetti launches into "herbs that rustle in the wind like sails," which does not convey the image of harsh difference that the original intends, as well as having a curious notion of herbs. I might have said "clutching grasses." It is a question of what image the translator sees in the original and wants to retain.

Giachetti does hit exactly the right note with her "elvish animals" where Le Guin uses simply "animals," Hughes "beasts" and Dana the technically accurate "little beasts." The Spanish word "bestezuelas" clearly implies a diminutive, and the "elvish" provides both the size and the idea that maybe these little creatures are able to communicate in some way with humans *a la* Narnia, thus "elvish."

This collection is not the complete poems of Mistral in English that we still await, but anyone who hungers for a broad selection of poetry from Latin America's first Nobel laureate will find a consistently readable and poetically crisp array in Le Guin's new translation.

Finally, one of Le Guin's best poems, "For Gabriela Mistral," in which Mistral rises from the lowlands and strides along on Andean mountaintops, appears in her own collection *Sixty Odd*, apparently inspired by her work on this translation. *Sixty Odd* is a fitting companion to her translation of Mistral.

Note: Le Guin's early masterpiece *The Left Hand of Darkness* (1969) was set in a world where residents became male or female as the need arose. Le Guin did not expressly include any variants outside male or female. In notes to a 1989 reprint of her 1979 essay collection *The Language of the Night*, Le Guin noted that "I quite unnecessarily locked the Gethenians into heterosexuality," which she viewed as a mistake. Her longer note on this subject is included in the 2024 Scribner reissue of this superb collection of essays on the writer's craft.

Darnell Moore: the Ebony Phoenix

(2019)

We are told that books should not be judged by their covers but by what is inside them. Darnell Moore's memoir[30] of growing up as a low-income Black person in a society managed by affluent whites is in fact exquisitely introduced by the charcoal lettering on its white cover: Black life as graffiti on a white wall. Faced with what appears to be an over-obvious theme, many readers, especially those like me who have never set foot in a black community of any size, may be tempted to nod, emit a familiar sigh and set the book aside to read later, meaning never.

What a loss that would be.

Some books, like some lives, are larger on the inside than on the outside. When we enter them we are *there*, experiencing life's realities at a level of detail that is exactly right. The gift of writing the truth this way, with its daily pains and victories, is given to Moore, or perhaps it would be better to say that he earned it the hard way. Yet many people live such lives and don't have the ability or social courage to make them real to an audience that is, at least in part, unlike them in life experiences.

I haven't mentioned the word "gay" yet because the first half of the book is foundation-building. It needs to be, and the deep networks of black life in urban America are laid out as much by example as by description. Why are they needed? Because this is the life of a remarkably complete, perceptive and self-aware writer, and he got there via experiences that we need to *understand*. Moore isn't telling only one slice of his story. We get all of the complexities of race, sexuality, and human relationships from family to childhood to college graduate. It's a rich and immensely rewarding plate.

Here we experience the manhood rituals of boys. Moore's complex father, who left the family but makes a bizarre reappearance late in the book, showed him how to swim (as did poet A.E. Hines's father) by essentially lowering the boy in eight feet of water and assuming that "the real, definitive boys and men stayed above the water and mastered the element that tried to control them." To sink "especially in front of your peers, was sissy shit." Those peers were a direct-action lot. Thinking teenage Moore was gay, they poured gasoline on him and only a failed match and a vigorous intervention by pugilistic Aunt Barbara, who happened to be passing by, kept the narrative alive, as it were.

About the time of Aunt Barbara's crucial arrival, the book starts to include a series of tension-building puppy-loves. Most of them are described with just enough detail that a gay male reader will recall similar events in our own growing up. The crushes, the doubts, the *sub rosa* fondlings, social denials and slightly "off" relationships with girls. These loves build in importance and richness over the years.

Moore's period of uncertainty and perimeter-building against his self-denied homosexuality was relatively long, extending well past his college years. It included a well-intentioned wallowing in old-fashioned religion before he emerged from that chrysalis, spent some time in a more formal seminary, rose from that fire, cast off any clinging bits of sulfur and found the light of God shining, or at least glimmering, in most people, a Quaker-like outcome that sounds simpler than it was.

Ever perceptive of unspoken truths, he notes in his explanation of how he came to his quiet faith that "the thirst for power leaves the spirit arid." In these days of religious lava burning its way through our society and politics, it is a rare privilege, even for a nonbeliever, to read the work of a writer whose spiritual core has so clearly been developed through a deep understanding of humanity.

In *No Ashes* we follow this development as we follow Moore's development as a gay man, as a family member and as a citizen of our troubled nation. They are one. During those transition years he came to recognize that "for many black boys and girls who are attracted to the same sex, black queer life is a life of solitary confinement" owing to the inability to talk about issues or questions with anyone.

The book's most universal and poignant chapter is called "Touch." I have never read a better series of expositions of what it actually feels like to cruise, to be touched, to have the experience of man-on-man contact for the first time. The gaze. The unspoken words. Contact and loss. This writing deserves a long life alongside the archetypal passages of John Rechy, Ned Rorem (whose sensation of having a young man hold him close as a teenager he memorably described as "a sheet of hot snow") and a few others who have memorialized gay men's emotions and the emotions of our time with such clarity.

One of the most important aspects to this story—one that the author clearly wants to emphasize—is the inherent vulnerability of young black men. With exceptional tenderness he reminds us that for society to recognize their full humanity, "black boys and men would have to be seen ... as bleeding, crying, vulnerable and sometimes resilient human persons" and not just as hypersexual masculine brutes valued and feared for their bodies, devoid of emotion and deserving short, rough lives. Moore notes with a rather fragile optimism that

> "Black LGBT people are not the amoral problems deserving of what has been inflicted upon us, nor are we victims who refuse to fight back or who sometimes die while trying. The more precise rendering of the problem is one that exposes both victimizers and an apathetic public that allows bias, violence and hatred to continue under its watch."

This book is not long. It doesn't need to be. Late in the story, Moore prepares for a long-postponed coming out to his mother. The book is worth buying just for the two heart-poundingly perfect pages this takes. Every word cuts a rising path from which the purest springs flow.

At one point Moore mentions a loose connection to the poet Essex Hemphill. This serves as a reminder that we have been graced by so much creative energy from Black gay Americans in recent decades that categories become irrelevant. Without even going to my shelves, Baldwin, Hughes, Robert Hayden, Reginald Shepherd, Carl Phillips, Jericho Brown, Alain Locke and Hemphill come to mind. Most of them are gone now but all of them produced work of quality. And that's just the men, and mostly poets.

A fuller look would certainly include Gwendolyn Brooks, Lucille Clifton, Audre Lord and several more poets, and composers such as Adolphus Hailstork.

Two of the men noted above have entered, or soon will, the rarefied canon of identity conferred entirely by literary surnames: we can say Baldwin and Hughes as we say Whitman and Dickinson and most readers will understand. Moore's writing is excellent, well along the way to a place with his great predecessors and contemporaries. A young life well written, and we're fortunate that Moore is still a younger man and may give us more in coming years.

Byron's Confabulation of Poets

(2017)

Reviewing John Lauritsen's *Don Leon and Leon to Annabella* [31] is in essence reviewing a review, as the book is entirely concerned with the meaning and provenance of another author's work. Lauritsen thus provides two benefits in one package. We get the full text of these two peculiar and interesting poems and also the assembled end result of an exceptionally thorough detective story involving the work of several serious researchers over a period of a hundred years. "End result" may be the wrong term for an investigation that has only a misty closure, but we get what is currently known, laid out in a way that allows any reader, even one not steeped in Byronic lore, to both enjoy the poem and appreciate the work of Inspector Lauritsen and his fellow sleuths.

Byron had a complex and somewhat troubled sexual life that would be recognized as a bisexual variant today. He seems never to have met a woman he didn't instinctively seduce—not that they fled from the handsome and charming writer. To the contrary, one of his more significant female companions pursued him ever more strangely for years, sometimes dressed as a boy. As James Merrill put it upon seeing a performance of *Otello* in which the understudy soprano stepped in for the final act, "Poor Desdemona! She changed the color of her hair, but it didn't save her marriage."[32] Byron was ditched by his one actual wife, apparently on fidelity grounds, after a very short time together. I can't help but wonder what credibility he thought he had by the time he wrote in *Leon to Annabella* of "all those I scorned" in order to remain loyal to Annabella. He scorned few.

But the words "he wrote" in that last sentence need to be explored. One of the main issues in this book is whether in fact Byron wrote any of this work at all. Lauritsen makes a plausible case that Byron probably did write the *Annabella* poem, though the story of its discovery in a peasant's hut once used by Byron reads like something from the annals of P.D.Q. Bach. *Annabella* has a masterful rippling cadence to it and is more readable and enjoyable as a poem than is *Don Leon*. It feels more personal than *Don Leon* and has some pointed, powerful, and delicately snarky language that we might easily use today despite the somewhat archaic style:

> Between the sheets salacious lawyers pry.
> Yet nature varies not:—desires we feel,
> As Romans felt; but woe! if we reveal,
> For what were errors then, our happy times
> With sainted zeal have registered as crimes.

By comparison to *Annabella, Don Leon* is really a sort of political brief dressed as a poem. A rather bald statement of the need for social tolerance of homosexuality, *Don Leon* is far ahead of its time, the first such statement known to be issued in English, though Bentham wrote something that was not published.

A much more direct, forceful, and in some ways cheerful ride than André Gide's austere, academic *Corydon* (1911) almost a century later, *Don Leon* feels more like Aaron Fricke saying in 1980 that he is damn well going to take his boyfriend to the prom, and society needs to get over it.[33] Not only is the tone unusual for its subject and time period, but the brute clarity of the message is akin to the opening of Stravinsky's *Rite of Spring*: a platter of radical, writhing new ideas simply heaved into the powdered face of the prevailing social order.

In addition to his more obvious and traditional hetero sex games, Byron took seriously at least one part of his early Calvinist upbringing: "God made man—let us love him," though in Byron's case God made boy. He had a taste for Gide-lings, though he quite sensibly approached writing of his uranic desires for teenage lads in a manner both oblique and coded, like the far more astringent and reserved A. E. Housman a century later. Whether he personally wrote these words in *Don Leon* can be argued, but their meaning, and the meaning of similar passages, can hardly be disputed:

Full well I knew, though decency forbad
The same caresses to a rustic lad;
Love, love it was, that made my eyes delight
To have his person ever in my sight.

Don Leon was published in one form in 1866 but written much earlier, probably in the 1830s or even 1820s, and most likely by several authors. Even if you know nothing of Byron the bisexual and don't care to, this work is an important piece of gay history. As a poem it is somewhat labored and quite variable, which lends weight to Lauritsen's view that it is in all likelihood the work of several quills, albeit in skillful hands, perhaps followers poetical, sexual, and temporal of Lord Byron: a dead poet's society, if you will.

So who wrote *Don Leon*? Lauritsen also published *The Shelley-Byron Men: Lost Angels of a Ruined Paradise,* which helps flesh out the nature of the group of young men clustered around the two poets in Italy. Speculation on how they might have collectively added to *Leon* appears in the *Don Leon* collection; the setting and relationships that serve as a principal basis for that theory are set forth in *Lost Angels*.

The response to *Don Leon*'s request for a new way of thinking about sexual variety was social shock. Early printings of this work were destroyed in one way or another, and the text became a rare and nearly mythical presence in gay history. As late as 1934, the London police treated a printing of this work as bonfire material, channeling their inner Mussolini. Whether these poems were by Byron, the school of Byron, friends and followers of Byron, or just courageous gay people determined to right a wrong, the poems themselves are a remarkable milestone of gay history, and we can all be grateful for their appearance in this exceptionally thorough source.

Andrew Marvell's Ploy of Sex
(2018)

What can a lay reader expect to digest from this dense and richly seasoned academic fruitcake of a book?[34] I suppose one could stop after the 27-page introduction, which alone has 78 footnotes and serves as a sort of encyclopedia entry on the subject of Marvell and the sexual content of his poetry and that of his contemporaries. The author, George Klawitter, has done a superb job of looking at what has been said on the subject of Renaissance sexuality—a very complex topic—and has added a broad yet detailed exposition of poetry of the era.

Klawitter has done everyone a favor by taking a nuanced approach to a colorful subject and giving the reader an opportunity to consider the full range of plausible views of a given situation. But make no mistake, this is ultimately a volume for specialists, a detailed library tour through the world of 17th-century poetry built around Marvell, a few of his contemporaries, and the various meanings of sexually loaded terms.

What are the author's theories about Marvell's sexuality? In a nutshell, the poet did not have romantic attachments to women, did not fall within "heteronormative" desire for any such liaisons, wrote about women from a chilly distance, and appreciated women's role in life from a somewhat clinical viewpoint. This is not to say that he couldn't write well about the male-female norm; he did so many times, sometimes on commission. Ultimately, the author concludes that Marvell had a "sexuality of one" and may not have been sexually active in the usual sense.

But what of Marvell's interest in men? It is to the author's credit that he has built enough of a factual foundation to conclude, with typical passing humor:

> "If Marvell were himself inclined to opposite-sex activity, a reader could not guess it from most of his poetry. ... his only real passion for another human being surfaces in one poem, 'The Unfortunate Lover,' and a reader would be

> hard-pressed to read that poem as celebratory of opposite-sex bliss or, for that matter, bliss of any kind."

We can hardly expect a respectable member of Parliament, which Marvell was for a while, to flaunt his homosexuality in the 1650s. The author suggests that in some cases he used the "safe and satisfying, if sometimes frustrating, ploy" of having words mean more than one thing, or perhaps several things, at once, as follows from *The Definition of Love*:

> Therefore the love which us doth bind,
> But Fate so enviously debars,
> Is the conjunction of the mind,
> And opposition of the stars.

Klawitter notes that we "are never told if gender plays a role in Fate's jealousy: she could be jealous of the narrator loving a man she wants for herself or she could be jealous of the narrator's loving a lady other than Fate." Complicating any explication of poems from this era is the problem of distinguishing sexual desire from "Platonic" love and an even more abstract category of "spiritual" love.

Marvell's slightly scandalous "Young Love" has attracted comment, referring as it does to an ostensible fifteen-year-old of unknown gender to whom an amorous poem is written. The author suggests an alternate interpretation having to do with the fifteen years Marvell had known King Charles, who was more-or-less a dead man walking at the time the poem was probably written. Recognizing that this interpretation is new and not obvious, he also points out, referring to Shakespeare's thirteen-year-old Juliet, that there's nothing in 1650s England to suggest that a 15-year-old would be considered ineligible for love, provided that we're talking boy-girl. The author speculates that "Marvell may well have lived a double life ... posing as celibate tutor to Maria Fairfax in the same year that he lusted after Damon, the mower of her father's fields."

One of the most rewarding parts of the book is the lucid, almost cheerful tour through "The Unfortunate Lover." The author sets forth various facts and theories about this arguably homoerotic poem, noting that "Marvell distances himself from only adult opposite-sex coupling, not all sexualities, because anyone who reads 'The Unfortunate Lover' should sense in the lines a strong and tender regard for another male." This poem can be remarkably physical, as the following extracted lines show.

Never was there human plant that grew
More fair than this and acceptably new ...
And his unimitable handsomeness
Made him indeed be more than man, not less ...
Lovely and admirable as he was.

See how he nak'd and fierce doth stand,
Cuffing the thunder with one hand;
While with the other does he lock,
And grapple, with the stubborn rock

Klawitter notes that "If indeed the poem is about a male ex-lover, one can only hope that the creation of the poem brought to the poet a therapeutic outlet for the feelings he could not share with friends or colleagues."

In addition to Marvell, this book contains significant material on many other writers of the period. Consider George Wither's poetic regrets from the 14th segment of "Miscellany of Epigrams," which reads in part:

But in our flesh we are, and must remain,
Perpetual strangers, and ourselves contain
From that embrace which marriage love allows,
Or else, I injure virtue, you your vows,
And for a short unworthy pleasure may
Those rich contentments which eternal are,
Of which I am in hope that always we
Should in each other's presence guiltless be.

The reader may be forgiven for thinking that the poet was in hope of something else entirely, yet defers to custom.

One of the strengths of this book is that Klawitter examines the subtle differences between Marvell and a few contemporaries in how they wrote about women—how warmly or detachedly. This is especially intriguing when the work of Marvell, probably celibate, is compared to that of other writers thought to be celibate but theoretically desirous of women. He is, for example, compared with poet Robert Herrick, whose work is presented as being more in sync with heterosexual literary conventions.

There are comparisons with other poets. Indeed, so many examples are set forth with such exhaustive care and thoroughness that we do not so much read them as check them off. The author writes very well, in an academic style frequently sprinkled with humor, but there's only so much one can do to lighten the burden of such an extensive set of literary sources written in the language of the 1600s.

The author discusses many other poems and even plays, such as Richard Edwards' (1523-1566) *Damon and Pithias*, an ancient tale that was exclusively about men until women were arbitrarily added in the 19th century. This detailed yet readable discussion is an example of how Klawitter shows where various writers got their ideas: Marvell is known for his "Damon" poems (perhaps related to the mower noted above).

As noted before, this book is probably not suitable for most lay readers, even those with a modest awareness of Renaissance poetry, for whom pushing through this forest of literary vines may well prove onerous. Specialists in this field, however, not looking for low-hanging fruit, are sure to learn something they didn't know.

Carl Phillips Releases *The Tether*

(2002)

Carl Phillips has built his presence in American poetry with measured confidence. The appearance of *The Tether*,[35] his fifth collection in ten years, provides an opportunity to examine a new body of work and gain insight into his themes and style.

What makes Phillips stand out from the pack? First, economy of diction, a restrained precision that displays the relative advantages of the scalpel as a poetic tool compared to, say, the leafblower of Ashbery. This attention to the true utility of each word recalls W. S. Merwin, especially his earlier work and such recent collections as *The Vixen*, but Phillips is less oracular and more rooted in the urban experience.

Phillips has a more natural acquaintance with a broader span of language than many poets, but he does not use a hundred-watt word unless it is the right word and the best word in a given line. If it is the best word then it fits perfectly and the reader does not stumble over an unnatural obstruction extruded athwart the poem's natural flow.

Although *The Tether* is more difficult than some of his earlier collections, he provides enough handholds that a reasonably intelligent and well-read reader can generate a meaningful vision from almost all of his poems. A good poem contains enough points of reference that the reader can understand what is going on and navigate through any uncharted waters, emerging at the end with a reasonably clear vision generated by words and, in the hands of the best poets, the absence of words.

Finally, for a poem to be worth reading it must have something at least mildly interesting to say: clarity in pursuit of vapidness, fairly common these days, serves no worthy master. Some poets seem to write about anything, in each poem Phillips clearly writes about something identifiable. He is a thinking poet, not merely a writing poet. There is gold to be found in these poems, and emeralds, velvet, steel, oak and cinnamon, layered and exposed in carefully-conceived chiarascuro, showing the reader enough that much more can be imagined.

I sometimes think of Cavafy when reading Phillips, partly because Phillips sometimes writes on historical themes or the ephemeral joys of men, but also because he finds and shows the reader links between our everyday lives and questions of spiritual and transcendent interest, witness the beginning of "The Figure, The Boundary, The Light":

> As he crosses the field, he is
> easily all I mean by the flesh
> is small, is occasional:
>
> the grass he divides with
> his body reuniting behind him
> like too immediate a forgiveness;
>
> even those birds that are least
> remarkable do not notice, and
> transcend him.

Even in this example of a field foray, there is little bucolic in Phillips: his outdoor settings usually relate to inward considerations. He is mainly a poet of indoor humanity and urban experience, but handled at viola pitch: even slightly seedy aspects of human experience glide well above street level for the reader to examine at leisure.

Comparisons are said to be invidious, but I like them because it is natural to want points of reference, so if you have not read Phillips and are tempted, imagine a more serious James Merrill whose concern with the soul is not based in a Ouija board and whose style is filtered by Merwin and you won't be far off.

Phillips is a younger American poet with the capacity to be one of the great voices of the century to come. If his themes and diction are occasionally reminiscent of Cavafy, Merrill, Merwin, McClatchy or Gunn, they are clearly his own in conception and situation—this is an original voice.

There are no crashing sounds in Phillips; the intense volcanic roiling characteristic of Reginald Shepherd (to name another African-American urban gay poet, if such a category means anything) is not to be found. Shepherd uses, if anything, an even broader palette of words than Phillips, but to read Shepherd (which I strongly recommend) is to be gloriously overwhelmed; to read Phillips is to be gently uplifted.

In this extract from "Spoils, Dividing," his delicate touch, concern with the relation of people to their spiritual universe and ability to hold a lot of meaning in a filamentous basket is clear:

How blame
the lantern whose limits

always are only the light of
itself, casting the light
out?

That the body enjoys
some moment
in that light, I regard

as privilege.
Say what
you will.

Perhaps this sense of uplift is the best way to describe Phillips. Even when he is describing loss, suffering, doubt or uncertainty (not his only themes, to be sure), I find myself glad that he chose to tell me what he has told me. There is a clear sense of having gained something from having read Phillips, and that is an uncommon characteristic among younger American poets today.

Returning to his first book, *In the Blood,* consider these lines from "On Holy Ground":

there is only the one sky,
whiter than any saint,
than the fire

they say will refine us all,

and your empty hands
that scrape it.

Phillips is always aware of that sky, reaches for it with hands that are never empty and, at his frequent best, leaves a gleaming platinum thread for readers to follow.

The Haunted Writings of Lionel Johnson

(2019)

Lionel Johnson (1867-1902) was a fey, elfin creature, so delicate in appearance that he was often mistaken for a teenager and "mothered" by various landladies and by do-gooders who imagined him truant from school. His writing, mostly poetry, was uniquely focused on the world as he imagined it to be, rather than as it was. This prompted his friend W. B. Yeats to write "he has renounced the world and built up a twilight world instead, where all the colours are like the colours in the rainbow that is cast by the Moon... ."

He took advantage of his unique appearance by playing female characters in local productions of Shakespeare. However, his sexual habits were, if not as cloaked in leafy subtlety as those of his near-contemporary A. E. Housman, nonetheless quite discreet compared to those of many of his friends.

Nina Antonia now offers us *Incurable,*[36] something of a pocket guide to Johnson. This small book is an illustrated biography (the first 75 pages) followed by a significant selection of Johnson's writings. The biography is detailed, masterful, gorgeously written, without a wasted word and packed with carefully researched high-quality gossip.

Johnson had a mixed relationship with literature when he was young. He noted that "As a child, I found one of my chief pleasures in pulling to pieces the Bible." Thomas Jefferson enjoyed the same pleasure later in life, but perhaps for different reasons. Johnson liked *Wuthering Heights,* Whitman (whose work he first read, aloud, while walking through an active cattle market) and Baudelaire. He was a friend of Aubrey Beardsley and of Yeats, who described Johnson and his friend

Ernest Dowson as "tragic penitents" as they toyed with the possibility of Catholic conversion and, in particular, of becoming monks, though presumably of somewhat impious habits. Escape from the world as we know it seemed to be their primary goal.

As an older schoolboy, one of his duties was to escort Lord Alfred Douglas to the headmaster "for a birching," and eventually he became "one of the leaders in a homosexual circle" at Winchester school. Johnson introduced his own love-interest Douglas to Oscar Wilde, thus playing a significant role in literary and social history. He quickly regretted doing so as Wilde, to whom Johnson was also attracted, quickly absorbed Douglas, leaving Johnson socially adrift.

The rest of the book features his poems, which are often quite moving in a fatalistic way. *A Dream of Youth*, dedicated to Douglas, includes these lines:

> Ah! How the fire of youth is fair,
> Yet may not be forever young!
> But night hath yielded, there hath sprung
> Morning upon the throne of night:
> Day comes, with solemnizing light:
> Consuming sorrows take to flight.

This poem, like many of Johnson's, is densely built, ornate, fairly compact and more or less traditional in tone and content for its time, though definitely high-church in its diction and objectives. Much of his work (indeed, much of his life) was disconnected from what we might call facts on the ground. His habit of mixing the actualities of daily life with his own constructed fantasy worlds became sufficiently well-known that even George Santayana noted their special effect:

> I returned often, and should have gladly have grown old in that atmosphere, yet not in order to indulge the impulse to dream awake: rather in order to remove the pressure of reality.

Santayana had a great appreciation for Johnson but also recognized that:

> He was a spiritual rebel, a spiritual waif who couldn't endure the truth, but demanded a lovelier fiction to revel in, invented it or accepted it, and called it revelation. In part like Shelley, in part like Rimbaud, he despised the world and adored the unreal.

The ageless, timeless, rootless Johnson eventually began drinking his way out of life, frequenting establishments such as the Crown pub, which though not a gay bar in the Twentieth Century sense (one wonders now whether the phenomenon was truly *only* in that century), functioned as a meeting place for his social cohort. He eventually died at 35 under somewhat murky conditions near one of those bars.

It is impossible to do justice to the exceptionally fine writing and research in this delightfully readable book. It must be read in its entirety to be fully appreciated. Johnson's absinthe-fueled sorrows fled early, leaving us a legacy of wondrous images that more ordinary eyes could not have seen.

The Danger of Uncontrolled Poetry

(2021)

The Editor of *Poetry* magazine, Don Share, was run out of town in 2020 after printing a poem called "Scholls Ferry Rd." by Oregon-raised poet Michael Dickman (not to be confused with his twin brother Oregon-based poet Matthew Dickman) in the July issue. The poem contains some racial images. I read it again to see what ghastly evil I had missed. It is laid out extravagantly over many pages, rather wasteful given its limited content, but is a meaningful poem. It's very clear that it is intended to be a reflective period piece describing how older members of a rather boring family think and talk. It succeeds in this.

Some readers responded with a Twittering to the effect that the poet's choice of words was wicked and made people upset. The effect of the complaints was that the Poetry Foundation produced a desperate, belly-crawling submission memo admitting that they had been bad. The *Times Literary Supplement* wrote that "In the ominous warning that followed – 'changes in the magazine's structure and process are imminent'– Mr Share read an invitation to present himself at reception at the nearest re-education camp."

What were the three awful, inexcusable words, the publication of which caused the leadership of *Poetry* to be instructed by the clacking Tweetbeaks to impale itself in the public square? "Negress" (an intentional archaism placed in the mouth of an ancient woman in the poem's best segment, about how white people think about and treat black people), "Hawaiian" and "Japanese." The horror, the shame.

Ridiculous. Adults do not need protection from poems. Are we really going to say that the world's poets should not use certain words because someone might be offended? Tell that to Neruda, to Mandelstam, Akhmatova, Ginsberg. To Ferlinghetti, who was still vertical at 100 when the Dickman affair occurred, charged long ago with a crime for publishing *Howl*. Speak those words to Essex Hemphill's steely ghost. This word-burning must stop. Are we to become a silent society, publishing nothing that a nine-year-old Baptist might not enjoy, out of fear of causing offense?

This kind of limitation is perfectly aligned with the approach of anti-gay politicians, for whom words are as great an enemy as acts. As gay people, we ought to be alert to any effort to deny a right to use unpopular words. Look at what is happening in Florida, Texas and other states where speaking about sexuality has become a political sin and therefore a legal risk. Look at Russia, where anything resembling a positive statement about gay people is now cause for imprisonment. Look at places where saying "I am gay" can result in a death sentence.

Literature is not a vehicle for ensuring universal happiness. Indeed, it is often intended to cause social churning, upset and, at a minimum, discussion. *Poetry* magazine held itself out for decades as the exemplar of good judgment in this context, the flagship, the pinnacle of what can be done with this literary form by our best poets. This mighty vessel capitulated easily, quickly and completely, its crew reduced to a quivering jelly, because of a tweet-spray about one middlebrow poem by a competent, standard-model career poet. The editor was invited to walk the plank on this questionable vessel and did so with an implausible letter of apology that is so steeped in subservient babble as to be risible—I read it as Share's parting expectoration, a parody *d'escalier*.

Even if *Poetry* had some positive intent (conflict avoidance doesn't count in literature), it is impossible to do what they claim they will and must do. It is not possible to predict what a given set of readers will find offensive or hurtful, outside the grossest examples. They will need a supercomputer to evaluate every possible nuance on their new Offensiveness Matrix.

Can a lesbian poet use the word "breast" in *Poetry* now? Can a male poet use that word? What if he's gay? Bi? What if they are trans? Can a Black female poet use the word "Negress"? Can a Black man? How black do they have to be? How will *Poetry* know, will each submission have to include a photo, melanin chart, survey and DNA test?

As a gay poet, am I limited to writing on themes related to my various physical attractions or the various oppressions, real or imagined, of my tribe? May I write a poem about a woman? A trans person? About birds or water? By blood I am one-quarter ethnic Mexican and ten percent Indigenous, so can I use the word "wetback" in a poem? What if I had personally crossed the Rio Grande in the water? What if my grandfather had? Do I have to send the editors my DNA test results to prove my ancestors were not really direct from Barcelona and thus not entitled to say wetback? Does my even greater Irish background entitle me to play word games with peat, potatoes and Popes? But wait, what if I am not Catholic? Or even Christian?

It can't be done. Neither *Poetry* nor any other literary entity should attempt to pre-screen other people's reading experiences except on grounds of literary quality, in which unpleasant words are not a disqualifier. Offensiveness is *always* unique and personal. It is never a legitimate evaluative point in determining quality. The Dickman affair is thus not a question of qualitative judgment, despite *Poetry*'s sudden insistence that it is, an obvious post-facto fogwall. It's a matter of denying adult readers a full range of literary experiences in order to avoid controversy.

The magazine has started a list of forbidden words. So far, words like gay, queer and dyke are ok. What happens when the board or staff changes? *Poetry*'s board has raised its murine forepaws in gasping supplication to a regiment of finches. Impure words are now Xd out by something artificial and hardly intelligent. Future submissions to *Poetry* must fit through the constricted mesh of an arbitrary, unpredictable and politicized sensitivity matrix.

One of Neruda's poems is entitled "Through a closed mouth the flies enter." *Poetry* has taped its own mouth shut and we already hear the buzz and smell the rot. What queer words will the world's richest poetry organization condemn out of fear of a chirp in the night?

The Gay Imagination

Part 2

Music

A Meditation on the Private Planets of the *Book of Mormon* Cast

(2017)

"Thank you. I'm glad you liked the show."

It's a simple thing, about as generic as it could be, yet something he could have avoided and didn't—a courtesy in a world where courtesies are getting to be thin on the ground. When "The Book of Mormon" came to Eugene I had the chance to see and hear the show thanks to a friend with an extra ticket. I sure noticed when they got to town—the gay dating apps that I used at the time lit up with a sea of new faces, many of which were visible on the stage that night. It seemed a little odd to use a dating app to say "thanks for a great show" to several men I could not possibly meet, let alone date, yet it was easy and my own courtesy to the performers who worked so hard to entertain us.

And they did work hard. Watching from the balcony with binoculars because the stage was so far away, I could see the sweat and the strain as the more energetic dance numbers ran their course. They do this night after night, week after week, traveling around the country. That is what it means to be a professional entertainer, the life that these mostly young people have chosen.

I found myself wondering what the life of A.J. Holmes, the off-brand hero of the show in the role of Elder Arnold Cunningham, is really like. It is clearly the life he wants—a quick look at his short bio displays that clearly enough. It's a short bio because this show requires a large number of very young men—they play Mormon missionaries, after all. Yet many of these remarkably young men (A.J. is well under 30) have an amazing amount of professional work stuffed into their short lives.

A.J. Holmes lives the life of an itinerant performer, which in the U.S. has the potential to lead to one or both of the only two things that are really valued here: fame and money. He seems pretty famous already, at least among those who follow theater, which I don't—Book of Mormon was the first stage musical I have seen since before Holmes was born. He will be a Star. Yet the life itself—touring the country constantly and gazing on passing faces in and out of dating apps—must be a strange and sometimes vacant experience.

I can't help thinking of the story *Songs of Distant Earth* by Arthur C. Clarke in which a spacecraft makes a stop on a planet before heading out to the far deeps of space. One of the crew meets a local woman and they fall in love. He is not at liberty to take her along. She is not free to go. They both realize that because the ship's speed is so high, the laws of physics dictate that when the ship stops again on its return trip—when they might both be free—he will still be young and handsome and she will be dead 300 years. I even wrote a poem about that story.[37] In a way, their lives represent the Unmeeting Wishes described in such lovely and excruciating detail by Austin Tappan Wright in his utopian novel *Islandia,* in which the American consul John Lang falls in love with the Islandian woman Dorna, whose destiny lies down another path.

Is it like that for the performers who tour the country bringing us colorful entertainments such as "Book of Mormon"? I have never toured so I don't know, but I can't help wondering what those dating apps looked like from the other side. Another array of potential perfect matches, another collection of young lovelies, yet what can they be but meteors passing against the endless emptiness of space?

I do not envy A.J. and his courteous stage-mates their fame or future fortunes. I hope that they find what joys they need on private planets where they return at the end of their tours to the quiet warmth of loved ones to whom fame and fortune are but dust among the stars.

Ned Rorem and the Future of American Song

(2006)

I am not sure why I did not come across the writing and music of gay composer Ned Rorem (1923-2023) until I was 47. I had seen his name occasionally over the years with no particular spark. A couple of years ago a reference to one of his diaries—I can't even remember where I saw it—finally registered with enough effect and I dug up a used copy of the *New York Diary* at a local bookstore. By the time I was 30 pages into it I knew that I would have to read more of them and listen to his music. I have now read many of his books and own several of his music CDs.

The recent release of both his latest set of essays (*Facing the Night*, Shoemaker & Hoard 2006), a collection of his letters to various famous and less famous people (*Wings of Friendship*, Shoemaker & Hoard 2005) and not long ago a collection of his earlier works (*A Ned Rorem Reader*, Yale 2001) provides an opportunity to look at his life works as a whole. I have to say "works" rather than "work" because Rorem, in his own words, is a generalist in the European mode, not an American-style narrow specialist. He does more than one thing well.

Rorem is frustrated at the prospect of being remembered more as a writer than as a composer. I lost track of the number of times in his writing that he declaims "I am a composer who also writes, not a writer who also composes." But that is not how history works, and history won't weigh in with any definitive trends for another twenty years or so.

It might be more accurate to say that his writing is likely to survive in toto as a body of literature read and discussed for decades to come, despite its somewhat repetitive nature, while his music is likely to be remembered in bits and pieces, with much of it fading out over time. Yet that is what happens to most composers and to most music. If it does not happen to all of his music and all of his written work, he will be among the rare few.

For example, who outside Australia knows well the gorgeous work of the late Colin Brumby, whose *Symphony No. 1*, flute and clarinet works and perhaps the *Piano Concerto* ought to be played by all of the world's major orchestras? Is Shaun Davey, whose *Relief of Derry Symphony* and *Granuaile* song cycle deserve great acclaim, a household word in the musical community outside the Celtic world? How many American concert-goers have heard the splendid *Sonata da Chiesa* of Adolphus Hailstork, from our own country? Who now hears performances of the Swedish master Ture Rangstrom?

Music is a world in which "modern" has become synonymous in the ear of many listers with "unpleasant," which leads orchestras wanting an audience into the closed loop of miscellaneous dead Germanic tunemongers, with an admixture of other dead Europeans (what to call them – a froth of French, a Russian roulade, a briskness of Brits?) and only the occasional living composer, generally the unpleasant ones.

There are exceptions to the rule of modern unpleasantness: in addition to Brumby, Davey and Hailstork, my mind quickly generates John Tavener, Jennifer Higdon, Arvo Part, Lee Hoiby, Einojuhani Rautavaara, Joby Talbot, Mary Ann Joyce-Walter and William Hawley. For that matter, we could, as always, do pretty well with film score composers such as Howard Shore, Rachel Portman, Randy Edelman, Ennio Morricone and Maurice Jarre.

Rorem is fortunate in that during his lifetime his music has been played fairly often, and some of his work that capsized instantly upon completion (e.g. his First and Second symphonies) has been refloated with considerable approbation. The Bournemouth Symphony recently released the first commercial recording of those two symphonies (as well as the Third, which had a brief life thirty years ago) directed by Jose Serebrier, and these works are astonishingly fresh and full of zing, a perfect blend of identifiable melody and modern intonation. This recording was nominated for three Grammys.

Rorem asks that he be first judged as a composer and I can say that I am very glad he is one, because his best works, e.g. some of those for flute, are likely to last for a while and have certainly brought me a lot of pleasure. That is all most composers can expect. Nonetheless, I think the diaries will, over time, be viewed as a unique literary masterpiece, burning in the dim corridors of historic time with a brighter flame than the music.

What is it about these diaries that makes them so appealing? There is a certain flavor of celebrity, of course, since Rorem fell in with a lot of well-known people in Paris, New York and elsewhere in the 1950s. Hearing of his interactions with people such as Jean Cocteau, Edward Albee and Leonard Bernstein, often when the Famous Person was not yet famous or was just getting to be known, has a certain sparkle. Rorem's willingness to state the, how can I put it, bare facts as he saw them, even when those facts are a bit more colorful or just more visible than what we usually see, adds spice to the overall tone.

Most of all, there is a sense of seeing sixty years of history open leaf by leaf, progress season by season. It is simultaneously a personal history, a history of 20th Century music (to be enjoyed alongside Alex Ross's *The Rest is Noise*) and a broader history of changes in American society, all at once, like the twining of cultural DNA from one horizon to the other, with some recognizable patterns but a lot of change and unique perceptions.

In its personal aspect, the diaries are also a history of gay culture. Rorem grew up in an unusual environment for the mid-century in that his Quaker parents were apparently not too troubled by the fact that he was gay, or at least accepted it with grace. It is interesting to compare his relatively open experiences to the more constricted social beginnings of contemporaries Gore Vidal and James Merrill. Vidal grew up inside the American political establishment, choosing to write for a living (a living that was a little sparse from time to time) rather than accept the horror of teaching. Merrill did not really have to work for a living (Merrill as in Merrill Lynch) but became a respected and prolific poet. Both became open about their sexuality in a rather careful, restrained manner, though Vidal wrote about homosexual attractions early in his career.

Rorem, on the other hand, wrote matter-of-factly about the joys and disappointments of his own activity chasing men decades before such revelations were common. He did not belabor the issue, it was just part of his life so it came up naturally in his writings without taking over the story. It is that matter-of-factness that makes these works stand out in the period in which they were written.

What I find most resonant about Rorem's diaries is his frequent descriptions of how the creative process works (or doesn't work). He does not discuss the process of writing music in much detail, but the various issues that any creative person faces, and the peculiar misconceptions of friends and family about that process, make for a table-pounding "right on!" sort of reading experience. The fact that I am also a gay person raised in Quaker meeting, as he was, makes this sense of having found a philosophical uncle all the more rewarding.

A good example of his perfect evocation of the necessities of the creative process can be found where he refers to a friend who thought that the sights and sounds of Morocco must have been a great inspiration to his work, since he did so much early work there while vacationing, in a manner of speaking, from his nominal residence in southern France.

In fact, the great advantage of working in Morocco, in addition to a Gide-like exploration of the joys of young male Moroccans, was that no one could find him or distract him there, so he could pull the shades against the glories of Morocco and actually get some composing done. This is precisely the experience and reaction that I have had and that many of my friends who write and paint have had, to which I can only say "preach it, brother Ned."

For anyone who wants to experience the extraordinary breadth of human experience, including the greatest joys and the most horrifying losses, through the eyes and ears of a great writer and great composer, read the sixty-year saga of Ned Rorem in his own words, and listen to the generations of songs, symphonies and other music that this unique American voice has brought us.

Modern American Song

Returning to the world of American song in which Rorem was the leading composer for many years, I listen and I hear a universe utterly changed, and yet there are niches in which song, in a form that Rorem would recognize, though different from his own, is flowering.

A few years ago I heard the University of Oregon's all-male singing group On the Rocks while driving home one night. Local station KLCC played their version of Dire Straits' *Romeo and Juliet* and I had no idea who was singing or where this amazing a cappella version of the song had come from. I called the station and they said that it was a local group called On the Rocks. The station had a CD but seemed to have no idea where it had come from or where to get it.

The next day I went into a music store near the University and mumbled something to the clerk about the song. Before I was finished with my incoherent tale of music found and perhaps lost, he said "On the Rocks" and got a copy of their debut CD off the rack for me. These CDs had been flying out the door all morning, and turned out to be the highest-selling CD for the store all spring. I personally bought a dozen as gifts and an additional fifteen for people at my office who had heard my copy. In an extraordinary violation of professional norms, I even called my staff into my office on some pretense, closed the door and played it for them on my computer's reasonably good speakers.

What is so special about OTR, as they are often called? When I first heard and saw them, the group consisted of nine men ranging in age from 18 to 22, and they sing songs. Well, so do lots of groups. Someone who had not heard them asked me "is that, like, barbershop?" Ah, no. In fact when I invited one of the members whom I knew slightly to the regional barbershop contest—held about five blocks from his house—he answered with great courtesy that he did not think any of the members would be interested.

College musical groups are common. A cappella is less common, and least common of all is for a group of young singers to make their own splendid arrangements of very recent popular songs—sometimes songs that had only been on the radio in the original version for a matter of months—retaining the original content of the song but adding their own unique silk and fire to produce something that the university's other singing groups simply describe with the phrase "they're hot."

Today there are other such groups nearby; I recently heard the UO women's group Divisi, Southern Oregon University's Dulcet and Oregon State University's Outspoken. Many other colleges have them: for an astonishing listening experience, buy a copy from iTunes of Leonard Cohen's *Hallelujah* performed by Northwestern University's group Freshman Fifteen. This, their own arrangement, simply assassinates most other performances—and there are dozens. Buy the whole CD. Groups at Yale, Cornell and Michigan have been especially good in recent years.

OTR has made their own arrangements of the song "Hear You Me," originally by Jimmy Eat World, "Demons" by Guster, "Street Spirit" by Radiohead, Cohen's "Hallelujah" and "In the End" by Linkin Park, as well as "Romeo and Juliet" and others. They have also recorded Gounod's "Ave Maria" and Billy Joel's touching "Lullaby." I had never heard many of these songs before I heard the OTR versions; indeed I did not know that many of these musical groups existed. Why not? Because I am, musically, an old person.

Even if I had known of them, I would not have listened to their music, simply because people do not generally listen to popular music except for that of their own generation and, if unavoidable, of their children's generation. Since I have no children, rarely attend concerts including modern song and do not own a television, there is no venue in which I would hear this music. So at the very least the transliteration effect of my local singing groups OTR and Divisi has allowed me to experience music that I never would have heard. Barbershop, which my brother sings and I enjoy in moderation, is essentially a fixed style. Its generational crossover is more limited than that of the collegiate acappella groups, which are the true transfer agents of modern American song.

Changes in the Role of Song

Rorem has commented that it is inappropriate to compare the new music of his generation (generally, the first half of the 20th century, perhaps including the 1950s) to modern popular music because the former is, if you will, classical, while the latter is not. Thus he objects to, for example, comparing Aaron Copland and Bob Dylan because of the nature of their music in a technical sense. I follow this argument and agree with it up to a point, but the question and its answer needs to take into account the changing role of music and songs in society.

My late mother was exactly Ned Rorem's age; she was born one day later. In her youth, adults knew lots of songs from earlier days as well as from their own generation, and in general young people heard the same songs as adults, whether they learned them or not.

My great-grandmother's Liberty Chorus Song Book, issued in 1919 by McKinley Music Co. of Chicago, was used by my grandmother's family and recently came to me. Its editor, Anne Shaw Faulkner, also author of "Music in the Home," closed her introduction to the Liberty Chorus songs with the following declaration about a man returning from World War I: "he will want to sing and to have his loved ones sing at home, at school and in all community gatherings."

These were not only pre-headphone years but almost pre-radio years, with limited offerings available. The first commercial radio station was licensed in 1920, only three years before my mother and Rorem were born. The phonograph, today almost an artifact, had just switched to "long-play" 33 rpm vinyl from hard 78 rpm "breakables" in my childhood. It was first patented in 1877, so two generations before my mother's had heard music either only as live performances or as families listening to early discs. Listening to music on phonographs required electricity (not uniformly available in rural areas) and quite a bit of effort since the discs were hardly compact: the older ones I saw at my grandmother's home were about half an inch thick and contained very little music, requiring multiple discs for even shorter pieces.

Today, members of the same family typically have separate musical lives, and the song, as the "high" art form that Rorem knew and wrote for to great effect, has largely been supplanted by the song designed to appeal either to everyone (often in the form of advertising jingles) or to a specific target audience (country, rock, rap). Loved ones generally don't sing together at home or anywhere else, let alone at community gatherings.

If a single vocal form that meets the esthetic needs of all generations can be found today, it is a cappella singing by truly creative groups like OTR and its collegiate compatriots. Once when I attended an OTR/Divisi show, the age range in my own contingent of about 15 people was nine to 83, and the entire audience reflected this astonishing mix. I do not see that cross-generational appeal (outside music schools) elsewhere in vocal music.

Reginald Shepherd and Robert Philen (see "A Conversation with Reginald Shepherd" in this volume) point out that the pendulum of music may be swinging back somewhat as parents who grew up in the 1960s and 70s are more interested in their children's music of the late 90s and early 2000s than was true for several previous decades.[38] This is a good sign if it proves to be true. Certainly I have come to love some of the music I hear from the teenage birders I take on trips: I would never have heard Josh Ritter, Train or Macklemore without those contacts.

Before OTR became well known at the University of Oregon, I attended one of their shows and stood in line next to a couple of college-age women. They had heard of OTR and a friend had invited them, but they had not actually heard the group. They were discussing the group and asked another person in line what kind of instruments they used. "None" was the response, to which one of the young women looked at the other in amazement and said "but what do they do?" They sing, and singing is not called the "first art" for nothing.

One of my former co-workers, who is retired and lives her musical life mainly within the classical and operatic tradition, attends many OTR and Divisi shows. Her favorite song in their repertoire is "Romeo and Juliet," with Jeremy Davidson's supple, downhome baritone solo, available on OTR's first CD. After she had been to a couple of their shows and was singing the song in the hallway, I asked her what she thought of the Dire Straits original, which is a favorite of mine. She looked at me and said:

"Who is Dire Straits?"

Yes, modern American song is different from that of Rorem's generation, but it is in good hands.

Soaring with Sparkbird: Stephan Nance's Songs of Joy and Survival (2024)

Queer songwriter Stephan Nance, whose recent music is released under the name Sparkbird, brings to music the kind of observational breadth and detail combined with expansive diction and lyrical clarity that we associate with songwriters like Phil Ochs, Coldplay or Leonard Cohen or poets such as James Merrill or Pattiann Rogers.

There are difficulties in discussing song lyrics by themselves, without the context of the music, as lyrics are, while often poetic in their underlying nature, as Nance's certainly are, not truly amenable to scanning the way we do with poems. The rhythmic realities of a song have enormous effects on how the lyric words are used and how they sound.

A few of Sparkbird's songs have specific gay or queer-related content, but most are expressions of their broad interests and observational capacity. Nance is knowledgeable about birds, enjoys birding with their partner (a "spark bird" is one that lights the fire of interest in birds) and manages to work bird images into a number of songs. This can take some doing—it is not easy to find a lyrical fit for a Glaucous-winged Gull—but they manage this with consistent success, e.g. in the lovely line *hush, hush, listen to the Varied Thrush!*, which is not only a smooth susurrating rhyme but fits with the sound the bird actually makes.

Love takes many forms, and some of Nance's most moving lyrics are, though grown in the garden of the broader gay experience, universal in both their beauty and emotional thrust. One of their earliest songs, "Spring," from the 2012 album *A Troubled Piece of Fruit,* offers exceptional musical delicacy combined with a piercing message, exemplified in these extracted lines:

> Spring, and still
> Leaves have not all fallen from the trees.
> Holding hands and skipping
> Stones across the river.
> Flowers open
> Wider than I've ever seen.
>
> You can see them too,
> If you hurry.
> You can see them too,
> If you come back to me.
>
> Spiral bound
> The pages that you wrote to me.
> In between the letters lies
> A secret that I'm meant to see.
> It has been a season
> Since I have seen the sea.
>
> But we can go there soon,
> If you hurry.
> We can go there soon,
> If you come back to me.

Listen to the song for the full effect of hope blended with longing and, ultimately, a recognition that loss is possible. Another Sparkbird song about a love that is not yet (quite) lost is the unique "Pompeii," a powerful, inspirational ride from the 2019 album *Look at the Harlequins*. An extract appears below.

In a previous life
I surely
Swept you off your feet
And carried you away
From the choking ash
And scorching heat,
To begin anew
Beyond the ruins of Pompeii
And to live
To see another sunny day.

On every list
Of things to do,
An unchecked box reminds me
That the task of saving you
Remains undone
And unbegun
And unfulfillable
Until the day we need to run
Until the day we need to run
We need to run—

In recent years Nance has been issuing mainly singles and extended-play songs for the current streaming market. Their song "November" has received over two million streams in the year since it came out. Another recent song, "Envy," may speak to many creative artists, though of course we deny having these thoughts. Here are some lines about the rainy season in Portland:

Rough time of year
Do you sit through it too
With that envy so strong
That you can't even move

I must confess
An embarrassing truth
Almost nothing can hurt me
Like thinking of you

You've got a beautiful home
Bestselling novel and effortless style
You enchant the people around you
They swoon when you show even the hint of a smile

Rough time of year
Does it darken the doors
To the lofty salons
Of the luminaries

I have known Nance for some years, as they formerly lived in my community and I too am a birder. They offered a few thoughts in a recent interview, following.

An Interview with Stephan Nance

(2024)

Queer songwriter Stephan Nance has been singing and publishing music since their college years at the University of Oregon. Their song "November" has received over two million streams in the year since it came out. Now based in Portland, they perform around the world. This interview was conducted by e-mail in April, 2024.

What songs have you come out with recently? Any consistent themes or are they varied?

My most recent releases are "November," "Sparkbird," and "Arboretum." "November" deals with trauma resulting from sexual assaults, "Sparkbird" celebrates birds while reckoning with the passage of time, and "Arboretum" is a kind of confrontation of the ghosts of my romantic past.

All three were written after a dry period of several years, using fragments of ideas I had written down much earlier, so they do feel interconnected to me. I had a list of dozens of ideas I thought were worth coming back to, and I pretty much worked through them one by one.

In what sense do you think of yourself as a "gay songwriter"? Anything beyond the fact that you are a gay person?

I think of myself as a queer songwriter and a queer person. "Queer" carries connotations of resistance to heteronormativity and challenges societal norms around gender and sexuality. It encompasses a range of sexual orientations and gender identities that lie outside of heterosexual and cisgender norms, including nonbinary identities and fluid sexualities that I identify with personally. I only use "gay" as an umbrella term encompassing a broader spectrum of LGBTQIA+ identities.

I like to think that I bring a queer aesthetic sensibility to my songwriting, influenced by my fascination with analyzing media through a queer theoretical lens. It strikes me as queer to write lyrics that are intended to be sung and heard as well as read and interpreted.

So much of what I write reflects on my personal experiences, and to me it's impossible to fully separate that from my queerness. On the other hand, every listener brings their own unique experiences to their listening. Maybe queerness is in the eye—and ear—of the beholder.

Though from a different angle, I imagine that if my singing voice and the assumptions that come with it were stripped from my songs, people would have a hard time guessing the gender—or even the sex assigned at birth—of their writer. Piano tends to be associated with women for various historical reasons, and most of the best-known piano-based singer-songwriters are cis women. And the lyrical content—the first-person, confessional voice, the themes and imagery, the particular flavors of angst and sensitivity—generally draws comparisons to women artists or to queer ones.

What other living songwriters do you admire and listen to? Any gay ones?

Some of the living artists I admire most (not a complete list) are Regina Spektor, Fiona Apple, Joanna Newsom, Janis Ian, Jenny Owen Youngs, Jesca Hoop, Annie Clark (St. Vincent), Mitski, Dolly Parton, Aimee Mann, Cosmo Sheldrake, Anjimile, and Neil Hannon (The Divine Comedy). Of these, the ones I know to be queer are Janis Ian, Jenny Owen Youngs, Annie Clark, and Anjimile. Some of my newer favorites are Madilyn Mei, Fish in a Birdcage, Rabbitology, and The Crane Wives.

Do your earliest songs still please you? Any special favorites? Any that you wish you had done differently?

I find the earliest songs really fascinating. They're a scrapbook of my past, and they show me how far I've come both as a songwriter and as a singer. Lyrically, a lot of recurring themes became established in the first three or four years of regular songwriting. "The Penny Song" will always be special because it was the first one I uploaded to YouTube, at the urging of my then-boyfriend.

For the most part I don't have regrets about songwriting choices, because each song just is what it is and there'll always be more songs. One thing I wouldn't do now is use words like "stupid," "idiot," and "crazy," because at some point it got through to me that these are ableist terms and I stopped using them. I don't judge myself for having used them, and they show up in such mundane ways, but they do make me less inclined to revive certain songs because those words feel inauthentic to how I express myself now.

Have you always written lyrics and music? How did that start? Were they part of family life? Did you just start on your own? Have any of your experiences growing up—say, before finishing high school—been reflected or featured in your music?

When I was a kid, my mom sang everything, just making up little ditties about whatever we were doing or whatever was going on around us. So I picked that up from her. I still remember a little song I made up in preschool about a craft project. A few years later, I was playing on my grandparents' computer and discovered that the word processor had a text-to-speech feature that sang whatever you typed to the tune of Grieg's "In the Hall of the Mountain King." I spent hours making up silly lyrics for it to sing, and figuring out how to influence the scansion with punctuation or misspellings.

Before I was old enough to start taking piano lessons, I loved going to the piano and trying to make up my own music, though I have no memory of what my results might have sounded like.

Throughout elementary and middle school I did quite a lot of writing—always prose, usually science fiction and fantasy. I think something about poetry made me nervous. By 7th grade I had become absolutely appalled at the idea of writing poetry, to the extent that when I was meant to write a poem for a class assignment,

I instead wrote an essay about why I refused to write a poem. At the end of the year the teacher gave out certificates to every student, and mine was the "Not A Poet But A Journalist" Award.

In 8th grade I spent half my days at high school taking honors freshman English, an accomplishment that basically became my whole personality for a while. For that class I had to memorize a Shakespeare sonnet and then write a sonnet of my own. That introduction to poetic structure made something click in my brain, and poetry very quickly became an obsession. I went so far as to compile my poems into a chapbook called "Through Severed Eyes," which in hindsight I find kind of hilariously dramatic.

In high school, my best friend was a songwriter, and it was so exciting hearing her recordings and seeing her perform. I liked improvising on piano, and I sang all the time, and I still made up funny little things with my friends, but never full songs. Then I found Regina Spektor's album Soviet Kitsch, and I started learning her songs so my friends and I could sing them in the choir room when we had free time. I have vivid memories of singing "Ode to Divorce" and "Chemo Limo" like that. I did the same thing with Janis Ian's "Between the Lines."

I think going through the motions of playing and singing those songs made it possible for me to envision myself writing my own songs. Around that time, I wrote a couple songs for a hypothetical musical that I never ended up finishing, plus a chorus here and there for songs I never finished.

I ran away from high school before graduating, and I didn't have a piano for a couple of years. During that time I wrote a lot of poetry, mostly as a way of processing my thoughts and emotions and experiences. Some of those poems I'd post casually on my blog.

The song I think of as my first "real" singer-songwriter song—a silly song about a boy, called "(Hey You) Samu"—was a cappella with hand clapping. Eventually my grandma got me a keyboard, and songwriting became my go-to activity for both self-expression and procrastination. I missed a lot of homework deadlines, but I wrote a lot of songs.

I can actually only think of one instance of an experience from before finishing high school being reflected in my music, in my song "Wooden." After I ran away from home, I ended up living with my grandparents for a while. My grandpa gave me a stone engraved with the word always, and I asked him, "Why always?" He thought about it and said, "Well, you'll always be Stephan. And I think that's a good person to be." The song goes on to say, "As long as you're doing no harm unto others, then you're always doing the right thing by me." That was another thing he said to me during this time, though it was in a different conversation.

Does a songwriter have any obligation to address moral, social or political issues? Most of your songs don't do this directly yet you clearly care about issues.

I don't think it's an obligation per se, and I wouldn't fault myself if I only wrote lighthearted bops, because the world needs all kinds of art.

Even if my songs don't always tackle social or political issues directly, they often reflect my values in more subtle ways. Some issues I view as running through my songs include destigmatizing experiences of trauma and mental health issues, showcasing biodiversity, and acknowledging the climate crisis. "Sedentary City" was written in part as a response to a shooting at an LGBT nightclub, and "White Appetites" deals with the Dakota Access Pipeline.

You have an exceptional capacity for detail and for using 'named objects' in your songs, for example specific birds or places or things. Where did that come from and what does it give you as a songwriter that a more generic songwriter lacks?

A large part of what I consider to be my queer songwriting aesthetic draws on the work of gay Russian poet Mikhail Kuzmin (1872-1936). My study of Kuzmin's poetry cycle "The Trout is Breaking Through the Ice" in college has had a lasting impact on my work, beginning with the song "Japanese Garden."

In an essay on "Trout," Lada Panova highlights Kuzmin's "signature proto-Nabokovian strategy," his use of intertextuality and chains of associations "to involve culturally advanced readers in solving intellectual puzzles." This and other interpretations of Kuzmin's poetry opened my eyes to the power of hyperspecificity — something I already appreciated subconsciously, and had maybe even used to an extent. But Kuzmin's work showed me that a limit on this didn't exist.

For a few years my mental health issues interfered with my creative work, and during that time I became a birder. Once you've tuned into birds, it's like seeing a new color, so when I began writing songs again, it was with a changed mental landscape. My earlier work had gone so far as to mention pelicans and even shorebirds, but now I was fully dropping names: Glaucous-winged Gulls, Turkey Vultures, Surf Scoter.

I love art that conveys a strong sense of place in my music, and specific bird references can do some of the lifting there. They can also help indicate the season, and emotion. But I see this specificity as serving my songwriting in particular. Generality has its own purpose that isn't less valuable. I imagine it all depends on the stories you're trying to tell. Not a lot of mainstream music contains such specific references, but that music is crafted to blend into settings where the lyrics won't draw too much attention.

In more recent years I've been drawn to Kuzmin's concept of "beautiful clarity," which heralded the dawn of the Acmeist movement in Russian poetry, though if I remember correctly his manifesto on the subject actually dealt with prose. In any case, the songs I've written in the past several years ("Blue Jay," "Disembodied Mind," even "The Light That Comes Through") have been less lyrically dense and chewy, though I continue to record songs written before this period, so my trajectory probably isn't as obvious from the outside as it is to me.

Why did you choose to use the name Sparkbird instead of your own for your music?

I should say first that a "spark bird," in the birding world, is the bird that ignites a person's passion for birds. At first I thought it would be an album title, then I wrote the song "Sparkbird."

Then at some point I heard Annie Clark explain that she chose to use the name St. Vincent because she didn't want people to see her name and think coffee shop singer. I mulled it over and decided that Sparkbird might serve a similar function for me. It felt ambitious and aspirational—a name I could grow into.

It wasn't necessarily that I thought people would associate my name with coffee shops. More that my name just isn't very catchy. It's a fine name, but the back-to-back N's make the first name and last name blend together, and the majority of people don't remember the spelling. It's especially tricky when touring in Japan or Russia, because the spelling doesn't make sense. That's alright if you're just meeting new people for fun, but not ideal if you want them to easily find your music or details about your concert.

Do music and lyrics flow together naturally for you in songwriting or do you do one and then the other?

Often the two come together to begin with, whether it's for a single line or a handful, and from there it tends to go back and forth until it's finished. If the song follows a more traditional structure, there's usually a point where most of the music is in place but some lines or entire verses need to be filled in. I take a lot of voice memos, and in those parts I'll either sing just the notes of the melody or maybe I'll mumble some possible words.

Sometimes songs do start with either lyrics or music alone. "Envy" started with music, it was just a pattern I found interesting. I took a recording of it and labeled it something like "dark interlocking piano riff" in Evernote. Then a couple years later I listened back to it and decided to use it as a jumping off point for a song.

Sometimes I start with what I think is a great idea, but after hours and days of hammering away at it I find out I'm stuck in a corner, or I end up going in a direction that no longer matches what I began with. There are a lot of "kill your darlings" moments.

In those cases, I might later find an opportunity to recycle the material that got scrapped. There are some ideas I've held onto for many years and eventually managed to find some use for.

How much of your own adult life appears in your songs?

I'm racking my brain and even my most speculative songs are based on personal experiences in one way or another. I don't think I've ever conceptualized my work as reflecting my adulthood specifically, but it's true that most of the autobiographical content I draw on comes from eighteen years old and after.

One aspect of adult life that I haven't really addressed in my work is sex. I'm sex positive and body positive, and I admire artists who celebrate sexuality in their music. Maybe someday I'll explore those themes in my songwriting.

What role does your partner Adam have in your musical work?

Adam is my first listener for every song I write. For so many years I would only play a song for him when I was sure it was finished, but in the past couple years I've become more willing to share works in progress and bounce ideas off him. He played a huge role in the production and arrangements on the "Incredible Distance" EP (2017), but since that project he's mostly been a listener and cheerleader and occasional roadie.

Do you have any musical or poetic heroes?

I've mentioned most of them already, but some additional musical heroes are Harry Nilsson, Leonard Cohen, and Joni Mitchell. A handful of poets whose work I admire: Elizabeth Bishop, Ocean Vuong, Audre Lorde, Maya Angelou, Emily Dickinson, Anna Akhmatova, Osip Mandelstam, Aleksandr Pushkin, Marina Tsvetaeva, Sylvia Plath, Mary Oliver.

What are you working on right now?

I'm wrapping up production on my single "Mayday!" and a demo of a song called "The Circle Maker." After this I'm planning to release a few more demos, likely including "The Light That Comes Through" and "Atlantisia." At some point I'll assemble some songs into an album. (Or so I keep saying.)

In late May, 2024 I'm headed to Calgary for a collaboration with Dustan Townsend, better known as Fish in a Birdcage. And this summer I'm going on a one-month tour opening for the marvelous Madilyn Mei all over the US (plus Toronto).

Shortly before "November" blew up, I finished a new draft of my young adult manuscript. I've gotten really encouraging feedback on it from my mentor H.E. Edgmon, but it does need some paring down before I can begin querying agents. It's hard to find the time for that kind of work in my current whirlwind, but I'm hopeful that I can squeeze it in this year. I've put so many years of work into it at this point, it would be a pity not to keep that ball rolling.

If you could hold a jam session with three other musicians, living or dead, who would they be?

Maybe it's because I'm a solo act, or maybe it has to do with playing piano, but for so many years I've thought of myself as someone who doesn't "jam." But not long ago I was staying with my new friend Jonathan Berry (@jbmakinmusic on Instagram) in Seattle and he wanted to play something together. I played "The Light That Comes Through" while he improvised on violin, and it was one of the most exhilarating musical experiences I've had in years. I'm hoping we can do it again sometime soon.

Mathias Kunzli has contributed percussion and drums to all the music I've released as Sparkbird (with perhaps a few small exceptions), but we've actually never played together in real time. That would be a real treat. Maybe we can make it happen when I'm on tour this summer.

Oh, my God, I would love to have a singalong with Dolly Parton. That's my final answer.

Alex Ross's *The Rest is Noise*

(2007)

Alex Ross's *The Rest is Noise* is subtitled "Listening to the Twentieth Century," and that is an apt if laughably understated description. This glorious book is a must-read for anyone interested in music, and also for anyone interested in the ways in which music affects and is affected by society. I am not a music critic of any kind, but I do listen to a fair variety of what is broadly classified as classical music, as well as popular and folk music centered around my own formative era. I know what I like and what I don't like, and for the most part I am content to allow such determinations to translate as good music and bad music.

To his credit, Ross does not tell the reader that a particular composer would do the world a favor by jumping into traffic, as James Merrill wrote of his wish that Schoenberg's piano would collapse mid-concert so the audience could flee, but rather sets forth the conflicts and changes in music from the late 1800s through today.

There are acres upon acres of fascinating cultural linkages in this book. The effect of jazz and traditional Negro music on Dvorak and various French composers may seem arcane and brutally old, but this week I heard the Eugene Symphony in my home town perform a set of traditional spirituals with the splendid young baritone Nathan Myers. The guest conductor, David Alan Miller, mentioned some of this history in his introductory remarks, and then proceeded to conduct a set of eight songs re-set with orchestra by eight different living composers.

When I saw this dangerously modern item on the program, I expected something that I could barely put up with between Smetana's "Moldau" and Dvorak's Symphony No. 8. In fact Myers was superb and the modern orchestrations were interesting and often gorgeous. Miller's comments could have come directly from *The Rest is Noise* and perhaps they did. History matters. History is relevant.

Also present are the excruciating political entanglements of Shostakovitch, the iconic swirl and unexpected political difficulties of Richard Strauss, the dark musical involvements of Hitler and his enablers, all in perfect balance. I have never understood the "why" of Schoenberg, atonalism and the strange unpleasant sound-splatter they caused and still cause in music, but having read Ross's history of this, I have a better feel for it. Some of it still sounds awful, but the reasons why we hear some of it even today are more clear. The late Reginald Shepherd persuaded me to listen to more Schoenberg and give it a chance, and I was pleasantly surprised by his opera Moses and Aaron. So perhaps there is hope for me. And him.

What Ross does better than many writers is create and maintain connective tissue. He recognizes the flow of key events and adds only those side details that really build the story. I am reminded of such books as John Keegan's *The Price of Admiralty,* Roy Jenkins's books on Gladstone and Churchill, Michael Barone's *Our Country* or Robert Massie's *Dreadnought.* The perfect blend of detail, consequence and insight is rare, and Alex Ross is a master. Just one example is his description of the Prokofiev opera "Semyon Kotko" in which "a change in Soviet foreign policy forced a revision of the opera's libretto. The signing of the Hitler-Stalin pact in August 1939 meant that Germans could no longer be depicted as villains."

The tone, however, almost always stays fairly light, with doses of appropriate humor, such as the inclusion of a scene in which American soldiers, not recognizing a bust of Beethoven, cause Strauss to grumble that "if they ask one more time, I'm telling them it's Hitler's father."

The long autumn sunset of Stravinsky, the long vernal sunrise of Copland, the clattering surge of twelve-tone sound and the late twentieth century advent of so-called "minimalist' composers such as Philip Glass are all here.

Ross is writing expressly about classical music, but toward the end of the book he begins including references to song and popular music. I hope that this is a teaser for his next book; little would be more worth anticipating than Alex Ross on the last 100 years of American song.

By way of epilogue, I sent Ross a thank-you note, together with a CD featuring the Symphony No. 1 of Australian composer Colin Brumby. Ross, no culture-snob, sent me back an e-mail saying he had never heard Brumby before, loved the symphony and did I have any more Brumby? I sent him Brumby's piano concerto and two clarinet works, with the composer's permission.

History is happening.

The Gay Imagination

Part 3

A Conversation with Reginald Shepherd

The Moated Castles of Today's Poetry (2008)

Note: This essentially unrevised essay is discussed in the following section of communications with Reginald Shepherd.

Recent commentaries by Reginald Shepherd, Ann Lauterbach, Adam Kirsch and Christian Wiman all include a concern about the tendency of modern poets, at least American ones, to write from an excessively personal viewpoint and to form hives that buzz in a similar way, heads in and stingers out, serving mainly each other.

Shepherd, author of the literary commentary *Orpheus in the Bronx* (Michigan, 2008) is one of the nation's best poets and literary critics.[39] He comments on his blog[40] on a book and essays by Ann Lauterbach, whose enthusiasm for modern writing is tempered by a growing concern that poets are clumping into identity-castles to the detriment of poetry as a whole, and especially the poetic audience. These clusters tend to write as though they are only poets of a group, not poets as individuals. Thus we have womenpoets, gaypoets, longshorepoets and other double-jointed po-beesten. As Shepherd points out,

> "Such fixations on labels and side-taking seem more prevalent in the online poetry world (certainly in the world of poetry blogs) than in the print poetry world, where things are much more fluid and flexible, though such compulsive territorializing and fence-building is far from absent there either."

Lauterbach's book *The Night Sky: Writings on the Poetics of Experience* (Viking, 2005) discusses, among other things, the concern that literary movements such as "Language poetry" or other identifiable trends can end up driving the poets, rather than the poets driving the movement. If poets move along in a huddled cluster behind a predetermined literary shield and don't go outside its penumbra as they write, are the poets really writing from what they have to say, or are they forming a series of moated guilds for the purpose of mutual support and protection? This kind of branding or commodification is part of what Shepherd discusses on his blog.

Lauterbach writes of this problem in one of her essays (from the journal *Diacritics*) with uncommon clarity and a calm dedication to what words really mean that has become rare in poetic circles of late:

> "The aspiring young poet begins to write in such a way as to invite a certain critical attention, to 'fit' her work into one or another critical category. This is the main function of being identified with a group or school, to draw critical attention that individual poets, not affiliated with a movement or group, cannot easily attract. 'New York School' or 'Language Poetry' are given brand-name status, commodifying and homogenizing, so that critics (and poets) can make general identifications and totalizing critiques without having to actually contend with the specific differences among and between so-called members of the group.
>
> Those not so identified are left out, often understandably embittered or confused, as the idea of an individual iconoclastic poet gives way to collaborative and tribal identities. Thus the marginalized world of poetry begins to imitate other identity formulations which increasingly govern contemporary academic, cultural, and political life. Frightened by exclusionary clubs, the poet ceases to identify herself with the essential margin from which a vital critique must come."

There is so much of importance packed into this lens-hard paragraph that I hardly know where to begin talking about it. First, there is the understandable desire of a poet (or any creative person) to attract attention to their work. This, in today's world of poetry, also necessarily means links to employability, publishability and whatever level of fame a poet can expect within the literary world (not much).

There is also the general problem of narrowness that grouping inevitably creates. I write poetry about the natural world, and many of my friends have come to think of me as a nature poet. There are some very fine poets who can fairly be classified thus (Pattiann Rogers and Mary Oliver come to mind), but I don't think of myself that way. The looks from my reader-of-nature-poets friends may get a little wide-eyed when they turn a page in my next collection and find a long poem about a 1944 naval battle off the Philippines next to a haiku about a college reunion and a dark reminiscence of my jury service in a child molestation case. I'm afraid my market placement as a nature poet is slipping.

Adam Kirsch touches on the problem of excessive narrowness in his recent collection of reviews *The Modern Element* (Norton 2008): "Today, the poetics of authenticity is securely established. ... Yet it should be clear by now that this poetics has thoroughly failed. ... The sound of the critical madhouse is a thousand utterly authentic voices, all talking at once."

What does it matter if you speak with an authentic voice if no one is listening, or perhaps worse, if they hear what you say but either can't understand it or, having understood it, wonder that you bothered to write it. Poetry needs to be more than just unplanned bleating: we can all make noises, but if the only purpose of your sound is to make yourself feel good or call attention to yourself, please spare us the distraction.

Finally, there is the matter of the "essential margin" and the idea of the critique. Movement-clusters in the world of writing almost by definition cannot abide critique except to the extent that another member may suggest better ways to carry the group's water to its literary destination.

This brings us to the fundamental problem of the moats, what lies within them and why it lies there. Do these moats protect a convent or a harem? It doesn't matter. In both cases the inmates are all serving the same master. It is not the nature of the group's master that matters, it is the existence of a master. A 'school' of poetry can be a master. A poet worthy of the name can have no master.

Shepherd's blog and Lauterbach's book discuss whether literary movements or styles can become a kind of commodity.[41] A literary movement can become a brand, to the extent that what its members produce is purchased by a definable group of people. In the case of poetry production, that group may well be each other, within or hovering on the fringes of that movement, head in and stinger out.

What a horrible idea, poetry production. In today's literary climate being a successful poet apparently means being employed primarily because one is a poet—that is, paid to be a college-based poet instead of having an ordinary life and writing from that experience. In this unfortunate context it's a natural term. There are rare exceptions but this is the normal, the common, definition of success.

Writing from a group identity rather than an individual identity generates a certain level of safety, protection, and an uncompromising commitment to adequacy. This is hivewriting: the hum is constant and the result a good nap. What it never does is produce excellence. However, in that it matches American society. We live in an age that is threatened by excellence, resists it (especially in education) and thinks any kind of clear statement of position contrary to the direction the bull is running is socially damaging (to the speaker) and unprofessional.

Poets by the hundreds have started building their careers by humping along familiar lexical tracks trodden deep with dust by the herds. It is sad to watch. They all want jobs as protected college-poets. They want their extra-large photo in *American Poetry Review*, which would be hilarious if it were not such a peculiarly American way of establishing virtue-by-celebrity. Imagine where we would be if we had spent our literary column inches gazing upon photos of, say, Auden, Spender and Bishop, recorded for history by Isherwood, that ultimate pre-digital recorder.

Many modern poets become part of artificial moated cloisters constructed so that poets can run around inside them squeaking to each other like rodents turning a wheel. To what end? Although I understand and respect James Merrill's statement that he'd rather have one perfect reader than write for the great mass of people, surely poetry written as a group member for the group is too incestuous to serve any but the crudest needs. The fact that the phrase 'career in poetry' exists as a meaningful concept in academe is cause for humor tinged with revulsion. But that is how poetry works in the U.S. today, in groups and with the same kinds of networks and cliques as appear in other employment clusters.

Christian Wiman, who spent several years as the editor of *Poetry* magazine, in his essay collection *Ambition and Survival* (Copper Canyon, 2007) offers a clear view of what has to change:

> I have long believed, though, that to be truly ambitious is to be alone. Wordsworth says that a poet must eventually forswear all aid and criticism of his work or his ability to discern what's real there, what is most and only himself, will become too debilitated to function. Aligning oneself with a group is not the same thing as seeking criticism, but there is a way in which such identification dulls this blade of solitude, makes it easier to believe in what you're doing, and thus easier to become complacent.

The net result of this self-congratulatory clustering is that far more people think that they are good poets than is actually the case. The fact that they do not have—and will never have—a readership outside their guild doesn't seem to affect their understanding of their fundamental status. They are chimeras flitting in the forest of their own imagining.

An astonishing number in poetry's legions are parading about unclothed but for their self-woven *corona graminea*. In their pride of cult they have forgotten that the grass crown of the legions cannot be self-awarded. Even the consuls could not award it. It comes in its own time, from the people who have seen with their own eyes the supreme acts which earn the honor. When we see writers crowned in chaff, let us say so. Let us award our grass crowns to poets of all schools (or none) based on their work.

Sources

The following section is extracted and adapted from the longer conversation included in *Song After All* (2013), a special publication I prepared as a fundraiser for the University of Oregon Creative Writing program in memory of Shepherd, who died of cancer before he could conduct a planned reading at Oregon. The deleted material is mostly technical issues and material by third parties.

Foreword from *Song After All*

by Robert Philen
(2013)

People, especially in the often over-specialized world of academe, sometimes think I'm scattered in my thinking and interests. I've written on topics of race and ethnicity; health, disease, and culture; gender and sexuality; music – from bebop to boy bands; Lévi-Straussean structuralism; alcohol; and poetry. I shared with Reginald Shepherd during our time together a broad ranging and voracious appetite for discussion and consideration of everything – and why shouldn't we be interested in everything.

Our conversations were free ranging, delving into our respective professional fields – Poetry, Literature, and English for his part, Anthropology for mine – but also circumambulating regularly through the fields of music, paleontology, politics, history, birds, and food. This freewheeling attitude toward topics of thought readily fit both our temperaments and perhaps our choice of professional fields – where in both cases we had gravitated toward fields where specialization is certainly possible but by no means necessary, and where a generalizing attitude can serve one well.

But neither Reginald nor I were/are actually scattered in our thinking. Despite interest in a wide variety of topics, we both shared a synthetic approach, attempting to draw connections between seemingly disparate things. This came across in Shepherd's conversations with others, here with his correspondence, or in his poetry – for example in his usage of Classical allusions and imagery alongside contemporary realities, including realities of gay and/or black experience.

There were also shared themes that oriented our coupled thinking on the wide variety of topics we set our minds to, including the relationship between discourse and practice. In relation to poetry and writing in general, we shared an interest in the relationship between writing, the world, and action in the world. Some of

Shepherd's critics frankly don't get his frequent use of Classical imagery – Why did he need the mythology to express contemporary gay and/or black experience? Leaving aside for the moment his aversion to seeing poetry as expression, seeing it rather as the production of an enduring aesthetic object with its own existence, it's true that Classical allusion isn't needed to express some version of black or gay experience, but to express what he wanted, it was, and it was no less "black" or "gay" for it.

In his autobiographical essays, Shepherd wrote about Modernist poetry and mythology and the Classical World (through the lens of Edith Hamilton, Robert Graves, Bulfinch and others) as things that provided for him, a young gay, black man growing up in poverty in the Bronx, what Adorno discussed as the alienation of one's alienation – providing him with a view, really his only view, of how things could be different. In other words, it was partly through Modernist poetry and Classical mythology that Reginald Shepherd was able to become a self-actualized adult black, gay man. So, how could these things not be part of his expressions of gayness and blackness?

Shepherd really had a nuanced, yet still straightforward stance on the relationship between poetry/writing, social position, and praxis. His view in a nutshell was that poetry or other art is inevitably shaped by the social circumstances surrounding its production, but that art is never wholly determined by those social surroundings, nor its meaning wholly reduced to them.

As I write this, I have recently been reading Enrique Krauze's book *The Redeemers*, about key intellectuals and artists in recent Latin American history. I am struck by the degree to which José Carlos Mariátegui stands as a kindred Latin American spirit with Reginald. The early 20th Century Peruvian Marxist philosopher and writer shared with Shepherd an outsider's view of the workings of power, and an interest in social justice, but also an absolute emphasis on aesthetic quality in and of itself and an emphasis on individual possibility. For both this entailed an ability to respect the work even of one's nemeses.

One thing we see clearly in Shepherd's correspondences is the respect he often held for works of individuals he sometimes personally despised. Shepherd's ability to separate feelings about the person and the person's work is all too rare nowadays. This ability on his part is no doubt linked to his cultivation of an aesthetic position emphasizing the autonomy of both the artist and the work of art, while the rarity of this skill is no doubt linked to the widespread tendency to reduce art to personal expression or symptom of the artist's biography.

We see all of these qualities and positions playing out in this series of Shepherd's correspondences with Alan Contreras. But also some of the pleasures and pains involved in staking out an aesthetic space and the social interchanges involved in the production of ideas. We see the creative process unfolding in the medium of these letters. Which is not to imply that the ideas are half-baked here. Reginald was always meticulous and substantive in his words in even the most trifling of conversations, though also witty, passionate, occasionally biting, ordinarily loving.

Introduction to *Song After All*

Alan Contreras

In one of his short notes, Albert Camus speculates on a dinner conversation with André Gide in which Gide gives this response to young writers who ask if they should continue: "What? You can keep yourself from writing and you hesitate to do so?"[42] Reginald Shepherd was fortunately not subject to any desire to stop writing; indeed quite the opposite. For that we can all be grateful.

This chapter[43] is intended to introduce the reader to its writers, particularly the late Reginald Shepherd, whose six books of poetry, two collections of critical comment and several edited collections form a significant component of modern American poetic literature. Reginald's death from cancer at the age of 45 affected me personally, although I never met him. We corresponded by e-mail for 17 months and I donated the funds to bring him to speak and read at the University of Oregon. He died before he could come, but those funds and additional donations were used to establish a student poetry prize in his name and memory at Oregon.

How best can we honor a poet by recognizing the work of another poet, and how can that unique gift, a poet's voice, be properly set forth for the view of history, other than through the poems? It is easy enough to honor an historian with a prize celebrating new work in that field, or a particle physicist by establishing the Quark Jockey of the Year or some similar clearly related award. But how should we set the criteria for a prize honoring the life and work of a lost poet? Unless that poet wrote about one thing or only in a single form, the life, the work and even to some extent the "voice" are quite varied.

Reginald's interests were broad; his work was eclectic in subject if less so in voice. His past, particularly the way he related to his mother and the places they lived, was part of his poetic habitat. So was sex: he was hardly shy about what he liked and how much he enjoyed it. In this he was closer to Ginsberg than to, say, Ashbery or Merrill among gay poets.

Less predictable, perhaps, was his awareness of and sensitivity to the natural world, given his urban origins. Jericho Brown notes in his introduction to Shepherd's selected poems[44] that "In each book, Shepherd reflects the beauty of the natural world through an understanding of that world as endangered." This may reflect both Shepherd's own interests and those of his partner Robert Philen, a birder who got Reginald out into the world of birds and nature.

I have to offer at least some minimal descriptions. Reginald's work—though we never met he always signed with his first name—was certainly borne aloft on the great wings of candor, so we can't have any prize winners who waffle, fudge or hide the toys. Nor can we have mere diction-divers who, upon surfacing, scatter words here and there to see what happens. One of Reginald's mentors, the great science-fiction writer and essayist Samuel R. Delany, would eat us alive—dead or not—if we honored something sloppy.

I once described Reginald's work in a review as having "intense volcanic roiling," but I'm not sure that helps guide a student writer. There are similarities between describing poetry and describing wine: the fluid of meaning starts with some clarity but rapidly widens into a turbid swirl of ungraspable sparkles.

We should certainly honor his breadth of emotion, which in turn reflected the life of a black gay man growing up in the Bronx and eventually passing through the University of Iowa and Cornell. Yes, but emotion is a genus, not a species. We all see and feel differently: Stephen Maturin reminds us that "the kinds of happiness are not to be compared."[45] Poetic emotion can appear in the urbane scrollwork of J. D. McClatchy, the high church pointillism of Carl Phillips, the mythic immersions of Cameron La Follette, the whisper-forest of W. S. Merwin, the forceful rush of Adrienne Rich.

It is sometimes easier to describe what a poet didn't do and didn't like rather than to classify his work into a poetic taxonomy. There are no pallid stones in Reginald's lapidarium, he had no time for the poetry of pathological personalism, he recognized that below a certain point economy of expression becomes chastity of imagination, he had no allergy to facts and he didn't geld any lilies merely because critics preferred parsnips—let the lilies show their stuff.

Reginald was a remarkable correspondent. He is the only person with whom I intentionally saved an entire e-correspondence, and those 120 messages, treated as letters, constitute the bulk of this section, as the best memorial I can offer in addition to the prize. Perhaps my retention of those messages was a premonition that it would end too soon.

One example of how multiple subjects could gracefully occupy a small space in his writing is this, a single message on November 19, 2007:

> "If I ever find out what "emo" means, I will let you know. I did a reading at Columbia University week before last and asked some of the students there, but didn't get a clear answer. I think it's music by "sensitive" but definitely straight boys who play guitar and may or may not wear eyeliner. Fall Out Boy seems to have something to do with it.
>
> I too came across Aqualung by accident, having seen "Pressure Suit" (from his second U.S. album) on TV and then backtracked to his first U.S. album (which is a compilation of two UK albums, which I might try to track down). I adore "Strange and Beautiful" and also "Falling Out of Love," as well as "Good Times Gonna Come" and "Another Little Hole."
>
> That's a good point about my colonization being the problem to begin with. Damned imperialist cancer! And now I'm partially decolonized. Does that mean I'm a dominion or a commonwealth or something, like Puerto Rico?"

Ultimately, his published work demonstrated with sometimes painful clarity the great canyon between those who play the instrument and those who play the music. Many poets never cross it. Reginald Shepherd played the music as well as anyone, and that's what we'd like the prize winners to do as well.

Reginald has now gone on the long and terrible way, to borrow an ancient phrase used in Theodore Roethke's *The Marrow*, and we who remain can honor him best by never forgetting what he really stood for: no halfway house for the intellect, no auto-referential academic priapism. The best, always, or why bother? It's a standard I rarely achieve, but I know it exists, and that matters.

In *Orpheus in the Bronx*[46] he noted that there is a mainstream of American poetry, "broad, sluggish and muddy" that offers "convenient epiphanies in prosaic anecdotes not interesting or shapely enough to be short stories." His own work, issued to date in six collections,[47] is never sluggish or muddy, and glutinous turbidity will not be allowed of the prize winners. Instead we will require purity, light, joy and truth of the kind that he displayed in one of his masterpieces, "You, Therefore," included in his 2007 collection *Fata Morgana* and dedicated to his partner, Robert Philen, which begins:

> You are like me, you will die, too, but not today:
> you, incommensurate, therefore the hours shine…

and ends:

> … home is nowhere, therefore you,
> a kind of dwell and welcome, song after all,
> and free of any eden we can name.

Let us recall Elliott Coues's definition of genius as "that union of passion and patience which bears fruit unknown to passion alone; to patience alone impossible."[48] Reginald's passionate genius outraced his patience as his illness progressed, and we are fortunate in that at least one posthumous poetry collection has appeared, along with the posthumously published essays in *A Martian Muse*.[49]

In the final essay in *Orpheus*, he answered the question "Why I Write" by saying "I write because I want to live forever," a straightforward and heartfelt restatement of Gide's desire to "have something secure against death."[50] The blooms of his genius are exsanguinated, but we can honor their living colors forever with as many Reginald Shepherd Prizes and other joys as those of us who knew him can imagine. This collection is intended to be part of that picture.[51]

Phil Ochs wrote in his spectacular song-poem "Crucifixion"[52] that "success is an enemy to the losers of the day." Reginald received his share of criticism from miscellaneous losers. That his name will outlast theirs becomes more evident with each passing season.

Letters in the modern world

This exchange of e-mail correspondence is called "letters" and it is, to a significant extent, the equivalent of letters formerly sent between literary friends and writers. There are many examples of such published letters and they sometimes vary greatly in tone and substance, even when originating from one writer, depending on to whom the letters were sent.

For example, the correspondence of André Gide and Paul Valéry[53] focused primarily on their lives as writers, travels and relationships with others, while Czeslaw Milosz and Thomas Merton[54] wrote about a wider variety of subjects, sometimes their writing but also the state of the world and what other authors had done. Merton, however, wrote with a much different tone and focus to his college friend, the writer Robert Lax, with whom he often exchanged casual and lighthearted chatter about sex and what food he was eating, although to be sure they also discussed literature.[55]

The unique loveliness of work that can be found solely in collected letters is illustrated by this excerpt from the Gide-Valéry correspondence:

> "At sixteen, we would have been able to wander over the roads together, we would have had the sea at our right, the lonely East at our left, and before us, at a great distance, some venturesome inn in which to try our luck at satisfying all those hungers.
>
> "At night we would have pressed our faces to the windows, to see families preparing for happiness; and we would have gone down the chimney into rooms that otherwise were too calm, and we would have frightened the

people who were about to fall asleep.

"In the morning, before dawn, we would have had a swim and we would not have had headaches."

André Gide to Paul Valéry, December 15, 1895.

If you read the letters of Federico Garcia Lorca[56] you will find everything from nearly complete poetic drafts to his unique wiry drawings to self-flagellation over the perceived failure of a particular work. John Jay Chapman wrote to an extraordinary range of people about politics, literature, religion, philosophy and the processes of daily life, though his flagellation was mainly directed at others.[57]

In the absence of significant assemblages of hard copy letters between writers and other figures in today's world, e-mail is in fact a significant source of information about the life and work of writers, artists and others working in the fine arts and other fields. It is, however, difficult to collect in an orderly way, often mixed with a spray of technical chatter between mechanical devices and rarely thought of the way letters are – or were, there being very few letters today in the usual sense that the word has been used historically.

Ned Rorem discussed the nature of this transition in the introductory material to his own recent collection of letters.[58] He also noted that it is very difficult to obtain permission to include all of the responses to his own letters, so only his were included in the collection. This does provide a legitimate historical archive, akin to that provided for some American historical figures in the "Library of America" series, but it does not offer the sense of interaction that can be had from seeing both sides of a correspondence.

James Merrill wrote that he enjoyed setting words spinning off each other like billiard balls,[59] and that is partly lost in a one-sided collection. That is why I have tried to include as much of the back-and-forth of our conversation as possible. I am grateful to Shepherd's partner and literary executor Robert Philen for his willingness to support this approach to sharing Shepherd's legacy.

This correspondence consists in significant part of e-mail messages exchanged between me and Reginald from April 2007 until his death in September, 2008. Within a few months of the beginning of our exchange, Shepherd began having medical problems, as I attempted to schedule him for a reading at the University of Oregon. These issues continued off and on for the 17 months of our correspondence, though he maintained a remarkable commitment to communication until a few weeks before his death, by which time he "belonged to this world only by courtesy," as Lord Moran put it.[60]

A few minor typos have been corrected and a small number of words have been added in brackets where the writer obviously intended them to be. In a couple of cases, private addresses have been deleted. The names of books and journals have been standardized, italicized and footnoted for the reader's convenience. A very small number of messages appear to have been lost and those places are marked when they are clear.

For purposes of this collection, some messages relating only to his appearance at the University of Oregon have been deleted. I have made no changes to the text other than to correct spelling or punctuation, even in situations in which I now cringe at my own writing or opinions.

In a few cases a portion of the "conversation" moved briefly either to my blog or his, or to a discussion of some other item posted online, often my essays in the higher education media or Robert's blog. Most of this external material is not included here for reasons of length, but is available in *Song After All*. The notion that electronic venues are somehow more "permanent" than traditional print books is, of course, nonsense.

The exchange set forth here covers a variety of subjects, but the bulk include Reginald's thoughts (and sometimes mine) regarding poetry, music, occasionally other branches of literature and the fine arts, the place of gay people in society, the mechanics of writing and of poetry readings, his upcoming books, relationships and domestic life.

The blog posts, essays and the like on the subjects that Reginald and I discussed, mostly literature and music remain available in *Song After All*. Most of these are referred to directly in the correspondence, a few are merely ancillary stage-setting.

The problem of getting outside oneself in some way in order to obtain the panoramic view necessary to determine what questions should be asked and their answers attempted is an underrated problem in all fields. It is at least partly a matter of training, in the inward sense of the term that is more common in, say, martial arts than in electronics. Our society does not encourage careful, evaluative observation of much of anything, let alone the self.

The British philosopher Michael Oakeshott wrote that

> "The world in which many children now grow up is crowded, not necessarily with occupants and not at all with memorable experiences, but with happenings; it is a ceaseless flow of seductive trivialities which invoke neither reflection nor choice but instant participation."[61]

This was written in 1975, the year I graduated from high school, before personal computers, laptops, cell phones, i-anythings, bluetooth, blueray or blue states, before much more than three or four TV stations were available in most places.

One of the common themes in many of these short writings is the importance of meaning conveyed by words alone, in this age of visual images. Words can be used to clarify or to hide meaning, to promote or discourage a thought or idea, to advance or suppress knowledge. Reginald cared passionately about the proper use of words.

Sometimes the power of words is conveyed through other images. I read Antonio Skarmeta's play "Burning Patience" some years before it was used as the basis for the movie "Il Postino." The story is about how Pablo Neruda's Italian mailman became a poet and, ultimately, was killed for being one.

Words have consequences.

The Correspondence

April 22, 2007
Alan to Reginald

Just a note to say that I enjoyed *Fata Morgana*.[62] I particularly like Narcissus to Echo, Turandot, Eve's Awakening and While the Temptations... I have all of your books and very much appreciate your work. I'm a birder and have written some bird books among other things; it is nice to find actual birds instead of generic "seagulls" in your poems (they seem a recent arrival - your partner's influence?) but surely an immature ring-billed gull sets a new standard! Some years ago there was an uproar in the birding community because in the movie "Jonathan Livingston Seagull," in which a particular gull was supposedly being followed, it not only changed age in the wrong direction but changed species.[63]

I look forward to reading Robert Philen's pieces, which I notice you have linked to on your web site. I am particularly interested in the music one because I recently commented to a friend that I had always disliked Gershwin until I heard a live performance of "American in Paris" several years ago. It seemed astonishingly different from every (disliked) recording I had ever heard, and far, far better. I can't say I have become a Gershwin fan, but now I feel like I understand what Gershwin is supposed to be, and appreciate the music for what it is.

By the way, I mentioned your gloriousness in one of my commentaries in *Inside Higher Education*[64] last summer:

> "Faculty at the great majority of schools are not really interested in color-coding their potential co-workers on a sepia-index wall chart anyway; they are interested in whether those co-workers are any good. Their departments don't care that Carl Phillips, Yusef Komunyakaa or Reginald Shepherd are black; their co-workers care that they are three of the best poets writing in the U.S. today. I hope that nobody at Old Dominion thinks of Adolphus Hailstork as "the black composer in our

music department;" they undoubtedly think of him as the composer who wrote "Sonata da Chiesa," one of the best pieces by any composer in a hundred years.

Anyone who tried to recruit these people away on behalf of another school would, I trust, be discreetly shunted off in another direction and told to stop poaching. This is not because they are of color, it is because they are of quality. It is not faculty of color that are such an important example to students of all shades, it is good faculty of color. And there are not enough of them being made."

Best wishes for your continued success.

April 23, 2007
Reginald to Alan

Thank you so much for your note and for your kind words about *Fata Morgana* and my other books. I've realized in the past several years that I'm rather of a landscape poet, and Robert, my partner, is an avid birder and amateur naturalist. He has taught me a lot about the particulars of the landscape and its inhabitants, avian and piscine, both in upstate New York and down here in Pensacola, including the birds at the feeders we used to have. It's been a fascinating new realm for me. I've always been interested in accuracy and in the ballast of fact, and I've always loved the names of things. Learning about these things first hand is only of the many benefits of our relationship.

I read Jonathan Livingston Seagull in the third or fourth grade, I believe. I knew nothing about seagulls, but I was very disappointed that I couldn't meditate or concentrate hard enough to teleport, or whatever it was that he did in the book. I'm sure that if I had known anything about seagulls, I would have [been] irritated by the errors you mention--I was a very pedantic child, and am still a stickler for accuracy.

Robert and I recently saw the Atlanta Symphony Orchestra perform The Rite of Spring, a truly overwhelming piece when heard live (you feel it in your body), and a totally different experience than listening to a recording. We saw the Pensacola Opera do Turandot a few years ago (the inspiration for my poem), a surprisingly good performance for a very small local company, and had the same experience: when Turandot sang "In Questa Reggia" (she was a very powerful singer), my whole body vibrated.

I read your piece in *Inside Higher Education,* and was quite flattered and honored to be listed with Yusef Komunyakaa and Carl Phillips as among the best poets in America today. Unfortunately, though, when I read the piece I was locked in a discrimination battle with the school at which I'd taught here in Pensacola for many years, first as an adjunct and then as a one-year visiting professor. (I got a settlement, enough to sustain myself for a while but insufficient to compensate for what was done to me.) So I felt a strong sense of irony as I read the piece, which obviously had nothing to do with the wonderful things you said, but with the contrast between those much-appreciated comments and the situation I found myself in. I am unfortunately unable to feel very sanguine about the position of black faculty in academia.

Thanks very much for writing and, again, for your very generous words about my work. It's nice to know that when one throws one's rose petal into the Grand Canyon (in David Wojahn's image of publishing a book of poems), someone actually notices.

all best, Reginald

April 23, 2007
Alan to Reginald

Great to hear from you, and thanks for writing. I'm sorry that you had to read my *Inside Higher Ed* piece under such unpleasant conditions. I read both of Robert's pieces, very good. I think one of the things that made the live Gershwin so much better than the recordings was that I could almost feel the air rushing out of the instruments past me, it was indeed a much more physical experience.

Before I forget, the University of Oregon has a temporary appointment in poetry coming up in the creative writing program. Not sure how temporary or whether it could morph into permanent; I asked my spies today and that is all I have back so far. I hope UO was not the northwest school where you had a previous unpleasant experience. I'm afraid the UO is sometimes rather clumsy in how it deals with "minorities." They are absolutely sloshing with Good Intentions. However, I have very good contacts there from my previous job and would be glad to fish for information if you have any interest. Not sure what Robert's professional situation is.

As for your work, my local bookstore has a standing order for new works by only three poets: you, Carl Phillips and J.D. McClatchy - who have little in common but speak to different parts of me. I buy Komunyakaa from time to time, and lots of others. Among the dead, I return most often to Auden and James Merrill. Among translations, Pessoa, sometimes Gabriela Mistral and, when I was younger, Neruda. I need to get back to Neruda sometime.

I also support poetry when I can. Last year I underwrote a friend of mine's first collection in a very nice small run. It seems to me that those of us who believe in the value of the fine arts need to take personal action to support them, not wait for somebody else to do it.

Have you ever read a poem - really a series - called David and Jonathan, by Byron Herbert Reece? From a book called *Bow Down in Jericho*.[65] Came out in 1950. Extraordinary. I am talking with a local artist and publisher about bringing it out in a joint illustrated edition with Pessoa's "Antinous," which as far as I know has never been issued in the U.S.[66]

I appreciate your comment about facts as ballast. I think that's exactly the right place for them. I enjoy the poetry of Pattiann Rogers, but sometimes I feel as though I am drowning in terminology and I lose the poem. I have an acquaintance whose poetry is often quite good, but in one poem he included the words "ootheca" and "blattarian," perfectly real words related to insects, but I prodded him for it in a review I did for one of our local mini-mags. What does one do with that kind of language, anyway? I got this little ditty in my head, after which the poem was hopeless:

I wanta put my pecka
Inside of yo' ootheca

I am a poet of quite modest gifts (see above), but I enjoy writing poetry. Doing it well takes considerable focus and concentration. I think I do better in essays. That may be partly a matter of habit and practice, as I have been writing a lot of essays in recent years because they pay, which poetry usually doesn't. Here's to filthy lucre !

Are you and Robert aware that there is a gay birders national e-mail chatlist? We host each other and organize trips, etc. ... There is a large clutch of members in Atlanta called The Gaggle.

I seem to have written a whole story here, so I'll stop.

May 1, 2007
Reginald to Alan

Dear Alan,

Thanks for your note, and sorry I've taken a bit to get back to you. I went to the emergency room with excruciating abdominal pains the day before you wrote, spent most of the next day sleeping, and have been feeling sick on and off (mostly on) ever since. I'm supposed to see a specialist tomorrow who will hopefully be able to find out what's going on and (more importantly) how to make it stop.

I'm glad that you liked Robert's pieces. I think that he's quite brilliant, but there's a slight possibility that I'm biased. :-) I don't see live music much, but especially for classical music, the physical presence of the music and the music-making is utterly incomparable with the experience of listening to a recording.

UO was definitely not the Northwestern school I was referring to in my race and academia post; that was Evergreen State College. UO certainly seems like a good school, but Robert has a tenure-track job teaching anthropology here that he likes and I couldn't ask him to give it up for a temporary position. Nor would we be willing to live apart even for a semester. I know that's not typical of academics, but I put my life first, and however I make a living (very badly, at the moment), my career is my writing as a poet and critic, not as an academic, though I would definitely like to have a permanent academic position, for the health benefits even more than for the salary (as an HIV positive person, access to health care is crucial for me). But I do greatly appreciate your thinking of me and mentioning the possibility to me.

I'm flattered to be one of three poets for whose work you have a standing order. I read with Yusef Komunyakaa about ten years ago, when I lived in Chicago, but when I saw him at AWP he didn't seem to remember me. Oh well. Actually, I read with Carl too then, and Kevin Young. I've not read much Neruda in a while, but I was recently listening to Samuel Barber's "The Lovers," which sets several pieces from Neruda's *Twenty Love Poems and a Song of Despair;* it's a beautiful piece of music.

I have never heard of Byron Herbert Reece. Perhaps, with the aid of the Internet (good sometimes for other things besides buying stuff), I will try to look him up.

I love facts and things and lists of things, and sometimes I have to remind myself to maintain a balance between loading every rift with ore, as Keats put it, though I'm using the phrase a bit more literally, and overloading the ship to the point at which it just won't float (pardon my mixed metaphors).

I am getting a bit tired and so will sign off for now. Take good care.

May 01, 2007
Alan to Reginald

Yow, that ailment doesn't sound like much fun. Granted, we do leave our bodies behind eventually (as a nonbeliever I find this quite unreasonable and distressing), but to live in a body that is biting back really seems unfair. Let me know when you are about to turn 50 (I'm 51) and I'll tell you The Truth About Your Upcoming Colonoscopy. You are what, 40ish?

Robert is a good writer, clear and understandable, which is appallingly rare among professors. I've added his blog to the very short list that I look at now and then.

Evergreen, oy. Quite a decent place, really, but so detached from norms that they sometimes think they operate in their own universe. If I may be permitted an improper joke (impropriety being one of my strengths), they're so Green they can't figure out what to do with any other color. UO is not as much that way, though there is a pulsing core of people in and around the university who go through life looking for opportunities to be offended, and who of course profess their tolerance for all. Sometimes they remind me of that old Phil Ochs song "Love me, I'm a Liberal." It's a scream if you've never heard it.

I'm going to attach my working copy of the hypothetical "special edition" of Pessoa's "Antinous" and Reece's "David and Jonathan."[67] It includes my own intro, which can be ignored as the idle vaporings of the uninformed, and the text of both. I find both of these extraordinary, in different ways. Reece has a peculiar old world village-prophet feel to him—I can almost smell oil lamps and a goat—which in clumsy hands would fall somewhere between humorous and unfortunate. I find his hands remarkably deft. Jonathan starts out plain, almost flat, and suddenly turns to pure fire on the page—I can't think of another poem that, to my ear, has such a huge transition in tone. Made me sit straight up in the chair and think "holy shit!" I would be very interested in what you think of his work.

I'm reading Edward Hirsch's *The demon and the angel*[68] now. So far very good. After that the biography of Neruda, which will take a while. Would you like to do a reading here maybe a year from now? I can probably arrange the swag to cover it.

Take care of yourself. We need more work from you!

May 5, 2007
Reginald to Alan

I am forty-four this April and have already experienced all too much of my body's betrayal. I try to treat my body right (I feed it good food, I exercise it, I try to give it enough sleep and rest, I avoid stress as much as I can) and it repays me with pain. I saw a urologist on Wednesday and he explained that I have uric acid kidney stones which, unlike calcified stones, can be treated medically, with potassium supplements to make my urine less acid and more alkaline. I've just started them today. I try to hydrate myself, but I am also embarking upon a project of constant hydration. I hope that these two things will take care of that problem. As for my constant fatigue, that still requires investigation.

Robert does indeed stand out from the pack, in just about every way. I'm glad that you're enjoying his blog.

I would quite love to do a reading at U of Oregon if you could swing the swag. I do quite like that word, "swag." It makes me think of money swaggering, which in our profit-driven world I suppose it does. …

I am feeling much better, but in part because I've been so sick and lethargic, have fallen behind on a ton of things I need to be doing and have no desire to do. Speaking of things I do want to do, I'm looking forward to reading the poems you sent me.

Take good care.

May 8, 2007
Alan to Reginald

I was fishing around in Robert's blog and found several pieces on music in addition to the one on live vs. unlive performances. I don't have his e-mail so am sending you a little piece that I did recently. It is nothing special but he might enjoy it.

I think the transition from family musical lives lived jointly (generally true until the early 20th Century) and today's utterly splintered musical lives in which parents haven't the slightest idea what their children listen to or why, is an underappreciated cultural change in American life.

May 8, 2007
Reginald to Alan

Hey Alan,

It's getting rather late and I need to go to bed soon, especially as I've had a very stressful and upsetting day. ... But, as I type while listening to Aqualung (a very good British singer-songwriter I've just discovered, who's given himself a ridiculous name), I am reminded by your message of conversations Robert and I have had about the fact that today (the 2000s) families have much less splintered musical lives than they did. Boomer and younger parents haven't stopped listening to popular music as used to be the case, say with the transition to adulthood in the 1940s and the 1950s, when one part of growing up was that you stopped listening to rock'n'roll or pop music, and largely stopped listening to music at all. Boomer and younger parents are not only still listening to the music they listened to in their youth, but are often also listening to the music their kids listen to, which these days is largely a pastiche of older musical styles, especially Eighties music.

Even a lot of the "new" music sounds pretty familiar to young parents, and a lot of kids listen to the music their parents listened to, from the Rolling Stones and the Doors to Led Zeppelin to Madonna and Culture Club. So I actually think that at the moment there's less of a musical generation gap than there may ever have been, at least since the era of recorded and broadcast popular music.

Just a few thoughts before bed. I will show Robert your piece.

By the way, I really would love to come read at the U of Oregon if it can be managed. I really appreciate your thinking of me.

Have a great night.

May 8, 2007
Alan to Reginald

Enjoyed your recent posts. I am often intensely inspired by a particular piece of music to the point that I play it many times over in order to get it completely inside of me, where it can serve as a sort of charged battery of inspiration to be drawn on as needed. I have lately played the second movement of Colin Brumby's Symphony No. 1 maybe 50 times in four months since the composer (an Australian) sent it to me.

I am slowly pecking away at a novel and that ten minutes of music provides a perfect aquifer to feed a particular section of the story: it flows at exactly the right speed in precisely the right direction with matching dynamics. That sounds crazy but it works.

May 8, 2007
Reginald to Alan

I too often listen to a favorite piece of music, classical or artpop, to inspire myself to write. I love your image of listening to music to charge the battery of inspiration. I really am going to bed now. Good night.

May 16, 2007
Alan to Reginald

What an amazing sound, [George] Barker. Sound seems the only correct word. Like standing in a wind tunnel full of words. Yowza wowza ! Another poet some of whose work feels close to this is you. There are not many poets who can harness this kind of word-storm and ride it through to the end.

Thanks for sharing this poet's work. I had never heard of him.

May 17, 2007
Reginald to Alan

I'm glad that you liked the Barker. Your image of a wind tunnel full of words is incredibly vivid and evocative—perfect for Barker. And thanks so much, again, for your kind words about my words. I'm pretty sure that just about no one has heard of Barker, which is one of the reasons I wanted to write about him. I don't do it systematically, but one of the things I want to do with the blog is bring underread writers to whatever public attention I can muster for them.

May 17, 2007
Alan to Reginald

I'll have to fish for used copies of Barker on ABE. I just spent a vast amount of money on the bound set of complete works of John Jay Chapman[69] (an American essayist I had never heard of until recently) as a housewarming present for my new study (former garage), so it will be a while before I buy many new books! But I can't live without books!

May 17, 2007
Reginald to Alan

I had copies of Barker years ago, then got rid of them for reasons unknown to me, and recently bought a couple again (his first book and that 1965 *Collected Poems*, which is the volume I used to have) on ABE, which had them for much cheaper prices than Amazon's used vendors were offering. I buy too many books, and too many CDs, but almost always used, because I am poor. The problem with buying used things, of course, is that too often they're not in the advertised condition, and then I have to raise a stink to get a refund.

When I was teaching I got a lot of books as examination copies. I can still get history and social science books that way through Robert (he teaches anthropology). I just have to let him know what examination copies "he" has requested, in case a publisher's rep comes by and asks him about it.

I've heard good things about John Jay Chapman, but have never read anything of his.

June 1, 2007
Alan to Reginald

Hi Reginald. Sorry I have not corresponded lately. I was birding in eastern Oregon for a week (plenty of birds, plenty of mosquitos) and am about to leave for my long-planned birding tour with friends in Alaska. That along with moving stuff into newly remodeled space has eaten all my time.

Enjoyed your recent blogs and Robert's. I find myself examining race through the lens of birding. I have lived mostly in small cities in Oregon, with three years in central Missouri. In my forty years of birding I have met (to speak with and know) exactly two black birders, one of whom, Drew Lanham, was visiting from South Carolina (I showed him a life Marbled Murrelet), where he is now associate professor of forest ecology, and the other was a teenager from Seattle, where he is the adopted son of a white mother, oddly named Sullivan but with a heavy German accent. He's still there, in his late 20s and still birding.[70] Two, in forty years.

People meet most of their friends and social companions at work or through shared interests. For that reason I don't meet many black people in Oregon (I would if I lived in Portland) although I did in Missouri. But in Missouri, with many bird clubs and events, I met no black birders at all. I know of none in Portland.

Why not? What is it about birding culture, if you will, that doesn't appeal to black people as a "class"? I have thought at least a little bit about the question of income and economic class. I don't think that's the main explanation, because I have known plenty of whitish people who are barely middle class and yet manage to get binoculars and enjoy the experience. I concede that most birders are in higher education and income levels. But higher-income blacks don't seem to take up birding or, indeed, get involved in other kinds of nature work.

Do you or Robert know any black birders? I'd be very interested in your thoughts about this. There aren't a lot of Hispanics, either, but there are some – mainly imports as adults (e.g. from Chile or Mexico), not Mexican-Americans unless they are of my subspecies: two generations downstream from immigration.

June 2, 2007
Reginald to Alan

Thanks for your note, and I'm glad that you've been enjoying my blog and Robert's. I'm really not a birder myself—I went with Robert quite a lot, but kind of burned out. A little nature goes a long way for me. Robert hasn't gone much in the past couple of years himself, because school has kept him so busy. I know that he'd like to do more. This summer he has a research grant and so isn't teaching for the first time, but you don't want to hang around in the woods here in the summer—the bugs will eat you alive, and keep on eating you once you've died.

I don't know anything about the racial dynamics of birding (neither of us has ever belonged to any organization), but I'm sure that they're murky and complex, like all things racial in this society. Class and race obviously are involved in the dearth of black birders, but how that mix plays out in that particular context I couldn't even begin to guess.

July 6, 2007
Alan to Reginald

Enjoyed your blognote on poetry about disaster.[71] The trick is to write *from* the experience of the disaster without writing *about* the disaster so specifically that the poem ages poorly.

James Merrill once said in an interview (I scuttled across the room to find it) that a problem with writing about current events is that "when the tide of feeling goes out, the language begins to stink."[72] I have always appreciated that view and the Merrilly twist to the phrase.

Hope all is well.

July 6, 2007
Reginald to Alan

Thanks for your note, and your very smart comments. Would you mind posting them as a comment on the blog? I like the idea of making such observations part of the public conversation.

Sunday is Robert's birthday. He'll be thirty-six. Did you see his post on crashing bird populations? Very depressing, and (especially combined with crashing bee populations) with scary implications for the human future. As the Checkers commercial says, you gotta eat.

Take good care. all best, Reginald

Blog comment: Alan Contreras said...

A literary movement can become a commodity, or at least a brand, to the extent that what its members produce is purchased by a definable group of people. In the case of poetry production, that group may well be each other, within or hovering on the fringes of that movement.

But what a horrible idea, "poetry production." I suppose in today's literary climate in which being a successful poet means being employed primarily because one is a poet—that is, paid to be an academic poet instead of having an ordinary life and writing from that experience—it's a natural term.

As for writing from a group identity rather than an individual identity, doing so generates a certain level of safety, protection, and what I am fond of calling an uncompromising commitment to adequacy. This is hivewriting: the hum is constant and the result a good nap.

What it never does is produce excellence. However, in that it matches our American society. We live in an age that is threatened by excellence, resists it, especially in education, and thinks any kind of clear statement of position contrary to the way the bulls are running is socially damaging (to the speaker) and unprofessional.

The great American essayist John Jay Chapman, who always knew bull on sight and which way it was running, wrote of the "general cowardice" of the age (this in 1900) and recommended a dose of truth thus:

> "Everybody in America is soft, and hates conflict. The cure for this, both in politics and social life, is the same, hardihood. Give them raw truth. They think they will die. ... The whole problem...is to get people to stop simpering and saying "After You" to cant."[73]

Chapman was writing mainly of how people interact in society and government, but the same problem—and the same solution—applies in the fine arts. An astonishing number of poetry's royalty are parading about unclothed but for their crowns. Let us say so instead of mounting up behind them.

Reginald Shepherd said...

I'm not sure that a literary community can be a commodity, but I definitely see how it can become a brand, marketing a trademark style to an audience expecting a certain kind of poetic "product." Obviously this phenomenon occurs with both "mainstream" poets and with "avant-garde" poets. Critic Vernon Shetley has written in the Irish journal *Metre* of "a poetry world where each poet seems compelled to enhance his or her brand recognition with an easily recognizable gimmick."

July 8, 2007
Alan to Reginald

I commented on your Lauterbach post. I'll have to dig up her book.

July 18, 2007
Reginald to Alan

I quite liked your recent column in *The Chronicle of Higher Education* on the problematization of knowledge and expertise. It was very witty and also very insightful. There was another article on that recently in the *Chronicle,* about how the Web has undermined intellectual authority. But in general kids today (I am so old) have a kind of contempt for the idea that anyone might know something they don't. About ten years ago a student in one of my classes said, in class, "You act like you know more than everyone else in the room," which I thought showed a remarkable lack of understanding of the basics of the pedagogical situation. I told her that I did indeed know more, about poetry anyway, than everyone in the room put together, and that she would have cause to complain if I didn't.

I was pleased to see you praise Merwin, who is a kind of eminence grise but not much read these days. I did a post about *The Lice,*[74] which I think an amazing book, a few months ago.

I did think, though, that you were too hard on creative writing programs. They're a popular and all too easy target, and while they certainly have problems, they're hardly responsible for the degradation of discourse or even of writing standards in this country. To the extent that they're part of that (which I think is exaggerated), they're only a symptom of a much larger cultural problem.

David Yezzi is sometimes smart, but, like most of The *New Criterion* crowd, he's much too self-conscious and self-satisfied a curmudgeon, and his aesthetic and intellectual horizons are much too narrow (perhaps deliberately, but it's no better for that). His anthology of newer poets is full of minor formalists whose only virtue is that they can (most of them, sort of) scan, which is good but hardly good enough. It's remarkable to me how many so-called New Formalists (Dana Gioia, for one) cannot scan to save their lives.

It's getting late and I should prepare for bed, but I've been meaning to write you for a while, and why put off until tomorrow what you can do today? Unless, of course, you just don't feel like it. Peace out to the homebodies and the homosexuals.

July 19, 2007
Alan to Reginald

I'm glad you like my "expert" piece, which was a lot of fun to do. I think your response to the student is exactly right: hey you little snot, you're PAYING me because I'm supposed to have knowledge to impart to you, not so we can all go on a shared-values picnic (slap, slap).

It is hard to know exactly how to approach MFA programs. I do think that there are too many of them, preying on students' mistaken belief that they can become "professional" poets. However, having access to good writers like yourself is hard to achieve any other way (I am very glad to see you taking private students). Certainly our society allows few other places where poets can, if you will, take shelter for a while and concentrate on their work.

The Lice is indeed great. My favorite is probably *The Vixen*.[75] His poetic style is so well suited to old places, old walls, old winds, old flames. Merwin, the poet of mystic recollection.

I picked up a copy of Lauterbach's *Night Sky* book[76] (my local bookstore tells me it is OP so I had to order it off ABE) and have started into it. It's hard to "read" because it is so unlinear, but there are chunks of pure gold within the swirling flow. Her command of language leaves me creeping along in the ditch, hoping to grasp enough words as they are tossed from her passing coach.

Did I ever send you any Colin Brumby music? I have his permission to share it with friends.

I'll talk to the UO people about your glorious visit when they are findable in August.

Homotextually yours, Alan

Alan to Reginald
July 19, 2007

Hey dude, I sent the formal request and offer of swag to Karen Ford, head of UO Creative Writing, today. Will keep you posted. If she doesn't like it, I have means of persuasion....

July 19, 2007
Reginald to Alan

Dude. Thanks for putting in a plug for me to come out to UO for a reading. It would definitely be cool to get to go out there, and of course to meet you. The swag would be nice too. I never get to swagger these days...

July 19, 2007
Alan to Reginald

With luck the swagman cometh. Actually the swagman arriveth a while back, it is the po-queen at whose feet I casteth my coin of the realm, no, wait, that's Carl Phillips's book, you're the OTHER living urbane black gay poet, where IS my form chart of these things, anyway? Gotta keep 'em straight. Well, aligned, anyway.

Did I ever ask you if you have read any Essex Hemphill? He's dead just now but I came across a collection of his.[77] Wow.

July 19, 2007
Reginald to Alan

Please, please, please don't confuse me with Carlo Phillipo. I have enough reminders that there's only room for one black gay classically inclined poet, and that he's the one. He's also been a pretty serious beyotch to me for many, many years.

And my forthcoming book of essays is WAY better than *Coin of the Realm*.[78]

I've read some Essex Hemphill, long ago. I was not so impressed. But I did meet him (and even go out dancing with him) when I was an MFA student at Brown. He was a very nice guy. I was sad that he died.

peace out to the homebodies and the homosexuals,

July 25, 2007
Alan to Reginald

Your e-mail hasn't been working lately.

I promise NEVER to confuse you with That Other Poet. Your writing certainly can't be confused.

UO Creative Writing program would be very happy to have you come talk to their little animals. Current director is Karen Ford. They can set up an evening reading and a Friday classroom discussion time with the 36 undergrads who are in what's called the Kidd tutorial - in effect their best students. We can probably add an additional informal kiss-the-poet session sometime. I'll see if I can get a local bookstore to have your books available.

July 25, 2007
Reginald to Alan

Thanks for your note. Are you sure you've been entering the right email address? I've been getting and receiving email without any problem, and even went to the webmail sites of my previous address and my current address to see if anything hasn't been coming through.

I don't like Carl Phillips as a person (I've tried over the years, but he's always been quite nasty to me), but he's written some wonderful poems. *In the Blood, After the Devotions,* and *Riding Westwards* are wonderful books, and *Cortege* is very good. I do feel that he's descended into stiff mannerism in recent years, and *The Rest of Love*[79] (which was a finalist for the National Book Award) was one of the worst books of poetry I've ever read, sentimental, platitudinous, and full of archaisms. He doesn't seem to be able to distinguish between his stronger and his weaker work, and neither does anyone else, at least the prize-nominating and -awarding anyones.

Thanks so much for wrangling this invitation to read at UO. I really appreciate it. Spring is fine with me, better than earlier in the year—I'd like to avoid weather related delays and cancellations as much as possible. ... I hope that you can line up some cute boys to kiss the poet. :-)

I also wanted to thank you for your very articulate comment on my Ann Lauterbach post.[80] I meant to respond, but I was feeling very depressed and overwhelmed for a while, and since I got out of it I've been swamped catching up on all the things I didn't do while I was in the slough of despond, like responding to the first set of packets from my California correspondence students.

I like *The Night Sky,* but the essays are rather disjointed; sometimes I wonder what makes them essays. As you wrote, though, there are a lot of gems to be mined. And I thought that Evan Eisenberg poetry quiz[81] you sent me was quite funny. I've read *The Recording Angel* (and hadn't known there was a second edition, which I will have to look up); I have *The Ecology of Eden*[82] but haven't read it yet.

Take good care, and thanks again for setting up this reading invitation. It's amazing to me the interesting people I've gotten to know, like you, and the opportunities that have opened up because of my blog, which I started by accident. I was intending to leave a comment on Ron Silliman's blog (which I no longer read, because it and especially the rabid attack dogs in his comments section upset me) and it took me to a page to set up my own blog instead. So that comment became my first blog post.

Poetic License Exam

By EVAN EISENBERG[83]

According to Code, spaces between stanzas must be
no greater than two inches
no less than one yawp
provided with a vermin-proof cap
filled with fine sand

Which tool should be used to disassemble a Petrarchan sonnet?
5-inch vise grip
31/2-inch strap wrench
Yale deconstructor
New Criticism

To prevent leakage, the lower end of a stanza of ottava rima (e.g. Byron's "Don Juan") should be sealed with
a couplet
a doublet
a stainless-steel cap and rubber gasket sleeve
duct tape

Enjambment is permitted when
space does not allow installation of a fixture on one line
a long-sweep 1/4 bend is used to connect the lines
a relief yoke vent is installed to vent overflow
a variance is granted by the Prosody Department

Which of the following should be used when a limited number of words are available?
single sanitary tee
double sanitary tee
3/4-inch copper sestina
limerick

According to Code, internal rhyme may not be used unless

it is installed at least six inches below grade
assonance is limited by local ordinance
metrical fittings are clearly labeled
a schematic is filed in the building superintendent's office

Which of the following types of rhymes or rhyme schemes does not meet Code?

macaronic
Hudibrastic
ABCB
PVC

To couple a line of iambic trimeter to a line of dactylic hexameter, the poet should use a

spondee
trochee
flange, gasket, and locknut
anapest, amphibrach, and 5/8-inch compression fitting

When essential components have been installed in an open-trench quatrain, any remaining space should be filled in with

extended metaphor
concrete poetry
reasonably clean backfill
hot air

The purpose of the trap in a canto drain line is to

hold water
form a barrier to sewer gases
insulate individual talent from the Tradition
prevent afflatus from escaping into the living area

If a tanka overflows, the poet should

relieve stress on weak syllables
replace it with two haiku joined by a 3/4-inch street elbow
check the cleanout for obstructions such as pleonasm or prolepsis
use a plunger

July 25, 2007
Alan to Reginald

I finished *The Night Sky*. A strange mix, to be sure, but I flagged a number of pages where glowing lights remain. I also recently bought a used copy of Vernon Shetley's *After the Death of Poetry*.[84] I am not a very literary person, let alone classically trained, but I gain a bit from these writers.

Tell me what kind of boys you like and I'll see what kind of kissers I can arrange! Yowza!

Phillips has either stopped paying attention or has become enamored of his own legend. Really too bad. Some of his work is sublime.

I am toying with a blog idea of my own and have set up the shell. Not sure yet whether it is the right way to spend my time. Sold essays to Chron of Higher Ed and Inside Higher Ed this week, and there is something to be said for working on things that generate revenue.

July 26, 2007
Reginald to Alan

For a non-literary person, you have a lot more literary smarts than many self-proclaimed (and self-assured) litterateurs I know and know of. I think that *After the Death of Poetry* is a very smart book. I don't necessarily agree with his choices of poets he thinks are interesting, but his thesis, that contemporary mainstream poetry is too easy, not too hard, and insufficiently intellectually engaging, is an engaging one, and he argues well for it. I drew on it for my post on difficulty in poetry.

I think that Carl was enamored of his own legend long before he had one. It is a shame, because at his best his work is marvelous and unique.

Again, I really appreciate your setting up this visit to UO. Thou swell, as the old song goes.

I have found my blog useful in numerous ways--in bringing me into contact with interesting people (again, like you) I otherwise would not have known or even known about, in raising my profile (I've gotten some publishing invitations because of it), and even in getting me work (not just the private correspondence students, but a visiting position in a low-residency MFA came my way because of the blog). And I think of most things I write for it as drafts toward a second book of literary essays. I certainly don't consider their appearance online to be publication, and I don't believe in wasting anything I write. But if people are willing to pay you for your opinions, by all means go with that instead. I suppose in part it depends on what sorts of things you'd want to write, and whether they would fall within the realm of your paying assignments.

I need to get ready to go to dinner—I've a hankering for sushi—and so will sign off now.

July 26, 2007
Alan to Reginald

I bought "Death Of" because you mentioned it and because I like James Merrill's work and am interested in what he says of Merrill. I have heard Merrill called a poet of surfaces,[85] which is true in some of his work, but there is more to it than that.

Sushi, that's that stuff that was once in the ocean, right? Never touch it myself but there is a good place near UO that I will take you to.

What I get paid for is almost all about education issues. That's good, but it leaves a number of universes open. It is the question of how to spend time that is most vexing.

July 28, 2007
Reginald to Alan

Congratulations on your blog, which I look forward to reading. I often post pieces or excerpts from pieces I have already published or are forthcoming, since there seems to be very little overlap between the online audience and the print audience, to the detriment of both (especially of the online audience, who at least in poetry seem to read nothing but each other—I actually read one person write that he only read poetry online, which I thought a damning admission).

July 28, 2007
Alan to Reginald

Only reads poetry online?! Good heavens. Well, that's better than not reading it at all. Today I rearranged the sidebars and listed some "recommended living poets" with links to your site and one other.

September 3, 2007
Alan to Reginald

Sorry I have been noncommunicative lately, I have managed to get all my deadlines piled up together, a bad idea. However, I also sold a couple of essays, which means a new tripod to replace the rusty old clunker.

In mid-Sep I'll formalize the arrangement and dates with UO, then later this fall I am going to donate all the swag to them for this appearance. That way I get a tax writeoff and you can work with one contact here (them) on the actual event. But I'll be in touch when your schedule is set so we can have dinner etc.

Alan
Nostalgic for Nixon....

On Reginald's blog, Alan Contreras said...

You may not have any of those other stacks of toys, but you do have excellence, and there are those of us scattered here and there, including those like me whom you have never met (yet), who recognized that excellence for what it was from your very first book, who have purchased every book since, and for whom your name is on the very short list of standing orders at my local bookshop.

I read very few blogs—who has time, especially with a day job and my own blog and publications to work on? Yours is one, even when I don't have time to comment as I should.

We look forward to hearing you speak at the University of Oregon in 2008! I might even wear my upper-crust bow tie!

September 3, 2007
Reginald to Alan

I wanted to thank you for your wonderful comment on my post "Working Class Hero." I was quite touched by it. I had been nervous about posting that piece, because it's so personal and so open to potential misunderstanding as either self-aggrandizement or self-pity, but I was very heartened by the positive responses I received, and especially that some people said that they felt inspired by it.

Thanks also for your comment on the Stevens poem, which is one of my favorites. I urge you to take Stevens off your shelf and read around in him. He has some utterly amazing poems. Some people think his work [*gap in original, see below*], but though there are some frivolous poems (mostly in *Harmonium*), I find that the fires burn more intensely for being banked.

Take good care, and thanks again. I look forward to finally meeting this spring.

September 3, 2007
Reginald to Alan

No need to apologize for being uncommunicative; I have been very so myself, partly because I've been depressed (as the onset of the academic job hunting season always makes me), and partly because I've been sick (horrible kidney stone attacks and a scare in which my urologist thought that I had kidney cancer—luckily, he now feels "98 percent certain" that I don't). I've also had several deadlines, a couple of which I'm just ignoring. Bad bad me.

I didn't realize that you were putting up the money for my UO trip. That's amazing and incredibly generous. Wow. Thank you.

By the way, in my previous message, I meant to write that some people find Stevens' work cold. That sentence didn't make any sense as I originally typed it. Bad me again for not proofreading more carefully.

Also by the way, the rat seems to have been [a] one-time sojourner, and Robert finally nailed a board across the hole in the garage ceiling, so I feel much safer and more secure. Around here at this time of year, an unfinished attic is a pretty uninviting environment for any warm blooded creature anyway.

There were some very depressing stories in the most recent Audubon magazine about the sharp declines in many bird populations around the country. I couldn't get myself to read them.

Take good care. It'll be great to finally meet in the spring. I may have already said that, but it bears repeating.

October 12, 2007
Reginald to Alan

Thanks for your eloquent comments on my blog, and sorry that I've been out of touch. I've been feeling rather depressed and overwhelmed, have been sick on and off (terrible kidney stone pains, which should be alleviated, since I recently had a lithotripsy to break up the stones), and also have been traveling (last month I had the worst and longest kidney stone attack of my life while traveling, which was particularly not fun). But I appreciate your good words, and thought I should drop you a note to tell you so.

I hope that you are well. Take good care. I'm excited about coming out to Oregon next year, not least because we'll finally get to meet.

October 12, 2007
Alan to Reginald

Good to hear from you, and hope that you have gotten your rocks off for good (that's a kidney stone joke, heh heh it will be funny in a couple of months).

I have done almost no writing lately except for work, though I had a call today from an outfit that wants me to do a turista guide to birding the northwest for them this winter. They are pretty well clamped down on my bait but they haven't talked money yet.

I'll talk to UO again next month and get them working on details. They are no doubt waiting for the money, too !

[a message from Reginald to Alan about a partial colon removal has apparently been lost]

November 17, 2007
Alan to Reginald

Greetings, o ye undead po-master! Let the Word go forth from every rooftop that you, prince-regent of the period and Count de Comma, are now a semicolon. But WHAT a semicolon !

Yes, I know, it will be funny in six months.

But in five months I hope to meet you. I just sent a note over to Creative Writing with my pledge of swag, and they will contact you to arrange something, probably in April.

I know you are probably tired these days, with hospital and carving, so I'll fade away. More later. PS check out the piece on online dating on my blog.

November 19, 2007
Reginald to Alan

Greetings to ye as well. I am indeed quite undead, to the point (not to mention the period) of being quite alive. Actually, the semicolon joke is funny now, though technically only a hemi-colon was removed. So I am, I think, at least three quarters still colonized. (A hemi is half, though, isn't it? I know less than that was taken out.)

Did you ever read the Dilbert cartoon in which Asok the intern convinces the pointy-haired boss that he should make everyone use semi-colons rather than colons to save space on the computers?

I might also mention that the Cancer Diet is an excellent way to lose weight fast. In case you were curious.

I got a note from Karen Ford regarding my reading out there, for which I am again very grateful to you. She said that the only available date in April didn't work for you, so we will do something in May, probably the 15th. I have teaching engagements all June, so I want to make sure to leave breathing room. It's so important to have room to breathe, don't you think?

It is indeed fatiguing being gutted like a fish, and I'm rather weary now, so I will sign off and go lie down. I took a walk around our suburban cul-de-sac with my sweet Robert, who is a whole panoply of angels, and am quite proud of myself for the exertion.

Take good care, and thanks for your good wishes. I look forward to meeting this spring. And I will definitely check out your piece on online dating [*see next page*]. I never did that, but I did lots of personal ads dating in the Eighties and the early Nineties, which was sad enough.

November 19, 2007
Alan to Reginald

I think the fact that you were colonized was the problem to start with! I had not seen that Dilbert, what a great one.

Glad Karen has been in touch. She is limited to Thursday nights, and she's not checking the symphony schedule, but the 15th doesn't have any big drawpieces so she's probably ok.

Never tried the cancer diet. I'll stick to being a fat person, thanks. Maybe worship St. Atkins[86] for a while.

More later.

The Ins and Outs of Online Dating

This note shows how quickly online dating and hookup activity on the Internet has changed. Most or all of the entities mentioned in 2007 no longer exist in 2024.

Some years ago, a friend with a dubious sense of humor mailed me a copy of *A Consumer's Guide to Male Hustlers* – to my office, in an ordinary envelope. The secretary displayed the calm professionalism for which we had hired her by opening and delivering this, as it were, disrobed object with my daily mail stack, offering no comment whatsoever. The book itself is a perfectly straightforward overview of the mechanics of hiring pleasure-boys and the nature of their profession.

Although I have never been in that particular market as provider or customer (setting aside the time when I, a college student, was offered five dollars to perform an unlikely act), I have wondered from time to time just what the less visible side of gay male dating was like. The advent of large, Internet-based databases for gay men to join and use as dating services makes the world of dating exceptionally broad, whether you are looking for Mr. Right or Mr. Right Now.

I recently joined a number of these services to see how they work and how they differ. I also attempted to arrange meetings with two men who provide what Craigslist matter-of-factly calls "erotic services"[87] in order to ask them how their profession works in the age of Internet-based dating. Historically, hookers and hustlers, mostly young, lurked on certain streets at certain times in order to find customers. Today it seems that at least the more upscale ones use the Internet to peddle themselves. Unfortunately one of the hustlers changed his travel plans and the other simply did not show up. I suspect that the latter was a student doing a research paper on people like me while I was doing one on people like him.

Joining the various services is easy. As a gay man, I only joined the ones that offered a chance to meet other gay men "in my area." It turns out that some of the services interpret "my area" to include the entire northwest rain belt: they gladly sent me profiles of "local" men from Seattle to Eureka. Of the services I joined, Dlist and

JustGuys are free, Manhunt has a nominal fee, Gay.com a higher fee, Elitemate pretends to have no fee to start with but is all but impossible to use as a guest and has by far the worst signup process. Men4Rentnow, which might be called a special-purpose site, and which I didn't use other than to look at its setup, has no fee. The general-purpose Craigslist is also free. There are lots of other services, but these seem to be the largest or most active ones.

These services vary greatly in purpose, ease of use and tone. Most of them are straightforward dating sites, though Elitemate seems to be mainly a bait-and-switch site designed to generate names and addresses for spam and the like, as is Naughtyornice. Both of these use bogus posts to Craigslist as bait. My test of their various signup sequences made that pretty clear, though I gave them mostly bad info and they are now sending a lot of messages into space, not to me.

Gay.com is one of the older sites and has a lot of men on it, but it is brutally commercialized, poorly laid out, has clumsy, sometimes nonfunctional controls for moving from page to page and includes a cute little trick in the registration process through which it hopes you don't notice that it reinstated a fee that the registrant thought had been deleted through an opt-out. In short, lots of guys but a real hassle to use.

DList and JustGuys seem to be connected in some way, though I did not spend any time looking into that. Both are fairly easy to use basic services that have pictures, info about the guys and minimal advertising. However, they seem to add members rather slowly, which means that when I want to meet Mr. Right Now on Saturday night, the available faces are pretty much the same ones (in my "local area") that have been offering themselves for some weeks or months. These sites are heavily used by college-age men, perhaps because they are free.

Manhunt is the best all-around service. For a small fee, you get a very well-designed, user-friendly structure that is all but adless, has plenty of people on it who really are in my local area (heck, I even recognized two of them), and does not seem to generate a separate spamflow. The site seems to have been designed by people who might actually want to use it, and flows wonderfully.

Craigslist is, in many ways, the most practical, and is an

increasing favorite among both gay and straight people wanting to generate dates in their area. It is also becoming a favorite way for prostitutes and gay male hustlers to promote their wares, as was discussed in an *Oregonian* feature article this fall.

One of the main problems I ran into with all of these services is that I don't speak the language very well. I'm a 51-year-old who does not own a television or a PDA[88] and whose cell phone is rarely on and used with minimal competence. The combination of gay sex-term babble and text-message code shorthand (shortfinger?) used by twenty-somethings often produces a homotextual sputtering that reads the way my Scottish ex-boyfriend sounded when he got agitated: only half the words needed for meaning are present on a canvas of apostrophes, and they don't mean quite what they would in standard English. Reading what people say about themselves (and what they want in a date) can be as clear to an amateur as FAA tower-chat or the more arcane marine forecasts of the National Weather Service.

But in all this world of linguistic obscurity, fake photos, unlikely measurements, no-show hustlers and unrealistic expectations, I did emerge from this experiment with one actual date, a perfectly delightful evening with a tall, dark, handsome 23-year-old. So my commitment to research has had, if you will, a result with benefits.[89]

November 19, 2007
Reginald to Alan

Just a short note to say that I was both entertained and informed by your post about online dating. What a Byzantine world! I thought that the world of personal ads was complicated enough (and at least half of my scheduled dates resulted in no-shows). Years ago I used to look at Hunk Hunter, which at the time was free and on which many people posted nude or even in flagrante photos of themselves, many of which one even wanted to see. I never tried to contact anyone (which might not have been free); I just downloaded photos. (I have about nine gigabytes of porno photos on my computer, which my Robert is kind enough not to make me delete.)

And now I really am going to bed. Peace out to the homebodies and the homosexuals, Reginald

PS--I also once had someone else's music library mysteriously appear on my computer via iTunes. I was rather disappointed that I could only listen to the songs, as she had several things I really wanted that aren't available anymore. You can go into "Sharing" under "Preferences" under "Edit" and turn off sharing. That's what I did, because I didn't know where this woman's music had been and what kind of viruses it might have picked up along the way.

By the way, Alice in Chains were an early Nineties grunge rock group, perhaps even from Seattle. I never liked them. I love Linkin Park, though, and "In the End" is my favorite song by them. Dashboard Confessional an "emo" act (really just one guy, Chris Carabbia or something like that, who's terribly cute) of the "Do me, I'm sensitive" school. I've seen a couple of their songs that I liked. As for those others, the lord only knows, and he doesn't talk to me.

I'm so happy that you like Aqualung, whom I adore. And it was nice to be reminded of Al Stewart; I always liked "Year of the Cat." Except for Imogen Heap, Steeleye Span, Stevie Nicks, Philip Glass, Phil Ochs (whom I've never actually heard), Indigo Girls, and Jimmy Eat World (whom also I've never actually heard), I've never even heard of the other acts you mentioned. Which I guess just goes to show that what they say about the balkanization of the popular music landscape is true. On the other hand, I realize that I have heard of most of the folks you mentioned. So what do they know?

November 19, 2007
Alan to Reginald

I had never heard any Aqualung until last month when I came across a gorgeous thing called "Strange and Beautiful."

Here's to hunks, long may they wave.

November 19, 2007
Alan to Reginald

By the way, what is "emo?" I see the term here and there.

"Be naughty, save Santa a trip."

November 19, 2007
Reginald to Alan

As you can see, I still haven't gone to bed as I should. If I ever find out what "emo" means, I will let you know. I did a reading at Columbia University week before last and asked some of the students there, but didn't get a clear answer. I think it's music by "sensitive" but definitely straight boys who play guitar and may or may not wear eyeliner. Fall Out Boy seems to have something to do with it.

I too came across Aqualung by accident, having seen "Pressure Suit" (from his second US album) on TV and then backtracked to his first US album (which is a compilation of two UK albums, which I might try to track down). I adore "Strange and Beautiful" and also "Falling Out of Love," as well as "Good Times Gonna Come" and "Another Little Hole."

That's a good point about my colonization being the problem to begin with. Damned imperialist cancer! And now I'm partially decolonized. Does that mean I'm a dominion or a commonwealth or something, like Puerto Rico?

This time I am going to bed. I swear.

November 19, 2007
Alan to Reginald

You are clearly a commonwealth. Good NIGHT now !

November 21, 2007
Alan to Reginald

Hey semicolon, when does *Orpheus*[90] come out? Can't remember if I mentioned that your Thursday eve event here will have a book table run by the UO bookstore. You don't need to lug any books. The norm is to have a signing after the reading.

I sent the swag to UO yesterday, so the deed is done and U B Cumin. Knowing you and your work is one of the high points of my life.

November 21, 2007
Reginald to Alan

Hey dear Alan, thanks for your note, and thanks again for setting up this reading. I'm very excited about it--it's nice to have something besides chemotherapy to look forward to. You'll be happy to know that after several days of what they call short-gut syndrome (in which anything one eats immediately takes the express train back out), my semi-colon seems finally to have decided that food, at least in small quantities, isn't an affront. I basically didn't eat anything the whole week I was hospitalized, so I guess it's understandable that eating again would be an adjustment. But I refuse to relinquish the benefits of the Cancer Diet (copyright applied for, patent pending).

Orpheus in the Bronx is coming out in January, knock on wood. That's what they tell me, at least, sans the wood-knocking. It would be great if you all had copies at the reading, along with my poetry books. I have an anthology coming out in January too (knock on more wood). I'm happy to sign books, before or after the reading. It makes them harder to return. :-)

Thanks for your incredibly kind words, by the way. I'm very glad to have gotten to know you too, if only virtually. You're an incredibly smart, interesting, and nice person. The blog has been an amazing thing for me that way, giving me the chance to get to know people I otherwise would never have met.

So the Internet is good for something besides buying stuff (though it's very good for that). It's also good for dates, too, apparently. I haven't been on the market in almost eight years, but I still reserve the right to be jealous of your date with a cute boy half your age. Did you get to second base? I hear those young ones are pretty randy.

November 21, 2007
Alan to Reginald

We rolled around in bed for a couple of hours; it was very nice. Not quite my usual type, a midwestern farm boy / linebacker type, tall and just slightly full-figured, with goatee, huge hands. And so very sweet and kind, which goes a looooong way in this world of snooty twinks and attitude connoisseurs. He even liked to hold hands !

He told me at the time that he was seeing someone on a regular basis, so I should not be too disappointed at his disappearance, but I am.

I see that Amazon is taking orders for *Orpheus*, which means my local bookstore (yes, we still have a couple) can order it now. I'm going to get one extra and drop it on the head of Creative Writing so she can experience your glory in advance of your arrival.

Enjoy your chemicals.

November 29, 2007

Reginald to Alan

It's nice that you got roll around in the hay with a cute young boy, and even better that it wasn't real hay, which would have been quite itchy and perhaps full of bugs. Holding hands at midnight, 'neath the starry skies—it's nice work if you can get it, and you can get it if you try. It's good that he told you ahead of time that he was seeing someone. I've dated guys whose way of dumping me (sometimes after standing me up) was letting me know that they were in relationships. Thanks for letting me know, chum(p). I can understand your being a little disappointed, but at least he didn't set you up for disappointment, the way I so often was.

Thanks so much for sending me those CDs, which I'm looking forward to listening to. You're a very generous person, in case you didn't know it.

I'm very excited that *Orpheus in the Bronx* is inching its way into existence. While I was in the hospital I got the spring University of Michigan catalogue including the book, which cheered me while I was in pain and unable to eat anything. I tell you, that cancer diet does wonders...

The chemicals haven't started yet, and I am not looking forward to them. I've heard nothing reassuring about chemotherapy from anyone. I have an appointment with my oncologist tomorrow to find out the extent of the cancer on my liver and the kind and duration (and side effects!) of my chemotherapy. I also need to remind him that I'm HIV positive, as immunosuppression is a side effect of chemo, and really I don't need any more of that, thanks anyway.

Speaking of doctors and HIV, I have an appointment with my HIV doctor this morning and should get going to that. Take good care, my friend, and keep the aspidistra flying. Whatever the hell aspidistra is.

November 29, 2007
Alan to Reginald

Hey semicolon, great to hear from you. I thought maybe some new music would help cut the dust of the trail, as we westerners say. We usually say it over something more easily poured (pourn? I think pourn should be a word, although I concede the possibility of confusion), but music will do.

Chemicals, diseases, various giblets. We are basically bags of saltwater with some, what is that delightful term, sweetbreads floating around inside. And we can only do what is possible with the terms and conditions that we are given.

Now, recall your liver to its duty by flushing it with perp-b-gone or whatever one uses on a recalcitrant liver.

My bookstore says The Book will occur in late January. Chemo will be nasty but you will get a nice lift from the book and will have all that behind you, and a freshly cowed liver (could I venture so far as coddled liver? Hmm, maybe not), when you come to Oregon in May.

Keep writing. That's all any of us can do.

December 1, 2007
Reginald to Alan

As Madonna somewhat ungrammatically says, music makes the people come together—music makes the bourgeoisie and the rebel. And anything that makes the trail less dusty is a good thing in my book.

As I was just reading in Richard Lederer's superficial but rather amusing *Crazy English,*[91] it's odd that sweetmeats contain no meat, while sweetbreads are neither sweet nor bread.

I saw my new oncologist yesterday. It was one of those situations in which the reality was actually worse than the anticipation. After telling me that cancer would inevitably kill me at some point, if I didn't die of a heart attack or get hit by a bus, he refused to say anything about the likely outcomes of my very heavy duty chemotherapy, or even to be specific about the potential side effects and how to treat them. I'll need to have a mediport installed (wow, I sound like a car), and will have three days in a row of in-office chemo every two weeks for six months (during which period my health insurance will run out, which should prove interesting).

My surgeon told me that the goal is to shrink the lesions on my liver so that they're small enough to be removed surgically, but the oncologist wouldn't even commit himself to that as a hoped-for outcome. Only time will tell, he kept saying, along with, Either it will work or it won't. I kept wondering, if we're just leaving things up to fate, why am I sitting here listening to you? But I'm just inquisitive that way.

Did I mention that I have none of the risk factors for colon cancer? (Just the opposite, in fact.) And that they don't even recommend colon cancer screening until age 50? Ugh.

I am definitely looking forward to the book of essays, and to my new anthology (did I tell you about that?), both of which should be out around the same time. And I'm definitely looking to my Oregon visit, even though my oncologist basically wants me never to travel because it might disrupt my chemo routine. But I'm not going to be a prisoner of my own body.

I actually started writing a strange poem/prose poem in section the other night at around two or three, on the little yellow post-it notes I keep by my bed. I've since transcribed it into my computer, but I'm not sure what to do with it yet. At that point, getting in and out of bed was still an effort, so this poem had better prove to be worth it.

Right now, I think that a little breakfast would be worth the effort of acquiring, so I will attempt to do so. - peace and pulchritude, Reginald

December 1, 2007
Alan to Reginald

Great to hear from you! Maybe we'll have to wheel you into the reading room on one of those tall carts full of drip tubes: The Mediportable Poet Will Now Speak.

Liver cancer is not good, but then life is always fatal. The only question is what we do with it. What you do is glorious, as the world knows. Well, a reasonable part of the world, anyway.

Maybe you should find out if you can get any really good stuff via your new mediport!

I just finished Christian Wiman's *Ambition and Survival: Becoming a Poet.*[92] Well worth reading. Images of poetry as a diving bell, for example. Major poets living in the suburbs of their gift and thereby fading. He, too, has a weird illness at a young age. I will do something on it for my blog sometime soon.

December 5, 2007
Reginald to Alan

I like that title. Perhaps I'll use it for a poem. I was never much for using the HIV shtick in poems, but maybe I can use the cancer shtick. (I do have a cane, after all, from some years ago when I had a knee inflammation.). L.E. Sissman got a whole career out of that. Then he died. But I guess everyone does at some point or another.

I would like to emphasize, though, that I don't have liver cancer, which I'm told would be very bad. I have liver metastasis of my colon cancer, which means that I have colon cancer that has spread to the liver. Apparently that's a much better situation.

This a fun week for me. Today I go in for a chemotherapy class, tomorrow I have my mediport installed or whatever the word is (I will then be officially a part of the Borg Collective--resistance is indeed futile), on Friday I see my oh-so-charming oncologist, and then on Monday I start my chemo. So much to look forward to...

Thanks again for your *tres* kind words, which are much appreciated. But wait. There's a reasonable part of the world? Why was I was not told of this?

Christian Wiman is an odd bird. He's kind of a terrible poet from what I've seen, and I've read some incredibly self-indulgent and self-involved prose of his in *Threepenny Review* and in *Poetry* (before he became editor). He wrote a very nasty and unfair review of my second book in *Poetry* many years ago but published a poem of mine there last year. And his wife wrote a vicious and comprehensibly ignorant review of my Iowa *Anthology of New American Poetries* [93] in *Poetry*, of which she's an associate editor. No nepotism there. I wrote an eloquently scathing response that seems to have intimidated her, as well it should have.

Meanwhile, I must call my surgeon's office about my medi-port. And eat some breakfast. Take good care, my friend, and talk to you soon.

December 5, 2007
Alan to Reginald

I'm glad you don't have REAL liver cancer, just an off-brand impostor. Good luck with your technical improvements.

More later, I have to go to the office (ugh). I will probably do a review of Wiman's book on my blog. And one of Alex Ross's absolutely magnificent musical history of the 20th century, *The Rest Is Noise*.[94]

December 12, 2007
Reginald to Alan

Thanks for your note, and sorry that it's taken a bit to get back to you. I had to go the emergency room (again!) this weekend, where I waited for eight hours to be seen. I've developed an abdominal infection/inflammation that had me doubled over on the floor in agony (wait, I remember that from somewhere, or somewhen). They gave me some antibiotics and I feel much better now (knock on wood), but it's delayed the start of my chemo, which is both frustrating and a relief. But I do just want to get it over with, and to find out what I'll be dealing with. Come Monday I'll know, or start to know.

I absolutely adore Alex Ross's book. I've loved his columns in *The New Yorker* and on his web site (also called The Rest Is Noise) for years, and I was so excited when I found out about the book. It's about the best book on music I've ever read. I'll be looking forward to your review.

Take good care, mi amigo.

December 20, 2007
Alan to Reginald

Hey semicolon, tomorrow is solstice day and a neewwww year is coming with all manner of good things in it including your glorious book and your Occurrence in Oregon ! So lick your chemicals like a good boy.

Do you have any interest in piggybacking an appearance in Portland onto your Eugene trip? Since you are done here Friday afternoon, we could look into a Saturday afternoon in Portland and a Sunday flight home if you have any desire. They'd have to pay your appearance fee but you'd already be here so it would not cost them any air, just hotel.

December 20, 2007
Reginald to Alan

Thanks for your note. Actually, according to my Defenders of Wildlife calendar, winter solstice isn't until Saturday. But I don't really keep track of such things.

I'd be delighted to go to Portland too as part of my trip out west. I've heard lots of great things about the city and have always wanted to see it. And if they're going to pay me too--well, all I have to say is, woo hoo!

So far the chemo is not so bad, though it burns my throat when I drink anything cold and today I got hit with crazy fatigue. I still managed to do my weight-lifting and my crunches, though I wasn't up to riding the elliptical trainer and it was _pouring_ rain all day, so I couldn't take a walk. They say that exercise helps with the fatigue and with the side effects of chemo in general, so I want to keep it up. Plus, I don't want to lose the svelte figure that cancer has helped me acquire--I weigh less now than I have in about ten years. I highly recommend the cancer diet to anyone who wants to lose a lot of weight in a hurry.

That's really cool that Alex Ross wrote you back. Somehow I'm not surprised--I've always gotten the impression from his writing that he's a nice and down-to-earth guy. Plus, he's a homo, which is always a plus in my book, unless you're a Republican legislator, in which case you're a lying hypocrite who should be taken out and shot. I will take a look at your piece on Ross. I'm thinking of doing a "my favorite books of 2007" post on my blog, which will _not_ include poetry (don't want to piss anybody off), but will include books like Ross's and this great book on the history of globalization, *Bound Together*.[95]

Okay, I just read your piece on Ross, which is very good. But I have to say that I think that you, like so many listeners, are prejudiced about Schoenberg, reacting more to the idea of his music than to the work itself. Schoenberg and Stravinsky were the first "classical" composers I ever heard, and it was they who made me decide that I liked the stuff. I've heard some "strange unpleasant sound-splatter" in my time (Robert listens to some free jazz, late Coltrane and Miles Davis for example, that sounds just like chaos and cacophony to me), and I don't have a great taste for what one critic has called "snarling dissonance," but Schoenberg's music just isn't in that category. And both Berg and Webern can be transcendentally beautiful. (Berg's opera Wozzeck is gorgeous and heartbreaking.) Anyway, I would urge you to listen to Schoenberg with more open ears. In exchange for the CDs you sent me, I'd be happy to send you some of my favorite (and more "listener-friendly") Schoenberg.

Take good care, my friend, and have a great holiday.

December 20, 2007
Alan to Reginald

I'll take you up on the Schoenberg offer. I have heard some of his work but not much. One thing I liked more than I expected, an opera (?) that I heard a couple of years ago. It was not Puccini, but it was musically interesting. Sometimes a challenge is good - we do hear far more Mozart than is healthy.

I got to hear the Berg violin concerto live a few years back, and although I can't say it would ever be a favorite, I got more out of it than I expected. Sometimes it makes a big difference to hear something live: I have only a very mild taste for Gershwin, BUT when I heard American in Paris live for the first time, it felt like a totally different piece and, although I'm not sure I'd admit this to just anyone, I kind of liked it. Shhhhh.

Let me see if I can get you a piggyback in Portland. I assume UO hasn't made your air arrangements yet? We might want an open-jaw ticket. It is GREAT to hear from you, drug-dude. Stay in touch.

December 24, 2007
Reginald to Alan

I hope that you're having a good holiday. I will definitely send you some Schoenberg, and maybe some Berg. All vocal, as that's where my preferences in all music lie. If you saw a Schoenberg opera, I'd think it would have to be either *Erwartung* (which is for a single singer and lasts about half an hour) or *Moses und Aron*, of which I saw a concert performance with the Chicago Symphony Orchestra conducted by Pierre Boulez. Sweet. We actually heard the Berg violin concerto, which I think is beautiful (and just a touch schmaltzy) down here with the Pensacola Symphony Orchestra, which is surprisingly good.

I don't much care for Mozart—it's all too la-di-da for my taste. I like many of Puccini arias, but there's a lot of cheese there too. "E lucevan le stelle" is incredible, though. Now that I think about it, in general I'm not much interested in the standard repertoire, and particularly not the standard operatic repertoire, which is pretty cornball to my ears. Just call me thoroughly modern Millie, at least when it comes to music.

Why would you be embarrassed to say that you liked *An American in Paris*? We also saw a semi-staged performance of *Porgy and Bess* down here, but the Bess was very disappointing. Overall, except for the Porgy, the cast wasn't that strong.

It would definitely be cool to be able to swing over to Portland while I'm out there. I haven't heard anything yet from UO about my travel arrangements, so I assume that there's still time. May certainly seems a long way off at the moment.

Take good care, my friend, and have a great holiday. peace and poetry, Reginald

December 25, 2007
Alan to Reginald

Ah, yes, it was *Moses and Aron*. Looking forward to hearing more. Do you like Ned Rorem's songs?[96] I just heard from Karen Ford this week. They will contact you in January.

We are expecting snow tonight. Actually not very common here on the valley floor and kind of a treat.

Have a great holiday !

December 28, 2007
Reginald to Alan

Thanks for your note and your holiday wishes. I hope that you've been having a great holiday season.

Moses und Aron isn't at all difficult to listen to, but it's a bit dull, especially when not fully staged. But then, how gripping can an opera about the conflict between two different conceptions of god be? I will send you some good stuff soon.

I love Ned Rorem's songs, though from I've read of and by him (including a nasty anti-Semitic comment in one of his diaries) he seems like a preening, vain, self-important ass. Luckily, I don't need to like him to like his work.

I'll be looking forward to hearing from Karen Ford about my trip.

I hope that you enjoyed your snow. It's impossible for me to conceive of such a thing as a treat, but then, I'm allergic to cold and snow.

Take good [care], and make a snowman or something for me. peace, poetry, and open ears, Reginald

December 28, 2007
Alan to Reginald

I think he IS preening, self-important and vain (unlike us). I confess that I love his writing; I have most of his books. His observations are sometimes quite good. I like his Sym No. 2 and a shorter work the name of which escapes me.[97]

January 21, 2008
Alan to Reginald

I read Adam Kirsch's recent collection of reviews recently.[98] It is an odd animal. He has real gifts as a writer, yet his reviews, for the most part, have a sameness to them, partly of style and partly of substance. He seems to have figured out what an Adam Kirsch review ought to sound like, and he pours Poet in one end and turns the crank.

I found myself feeling slightly undernourished by the time I was done, although his basic dislike of incomprehensible modern poetry is certainly congenial. Of course, he doesn't think much of James Merrill, whose work I like very much, and he likes at least some of Simic, whose work I can't get through.

Looking forward to your book.

I hope all is well with you.

January 21, 2008
Reginald to Alan

I've read enough of Kirsch's reviews that I don't think that I could bear a whole book of them. He tends to make sweeping and usually dismissive comments based on a sometimes shocking ignorance. He's definitely very into being "Adam Kirsch," which is not a very interesting thing to be. As for "incomprehensible modern poetry," I'm not sure what you mean (or what he means). I like a lot of poetry that might be considered such a thing. I even write a lot of poetry that might be considered such (some people think it is). Who do you mean?

I'm sort of surprised that Kirsch dislikes Merrill (who is sometimes interesting, though the being very rich grates on me, as do the highly disturbing social ideas in *The Changing Light at Sandover*[99]—not to mention the ridiculous Ouija board nonsense) and like Simic (except that I find Simic rather dull, which would work for Kirsch).

I just got an email from the folks at the very small, new press that's publishing my new anthology, *Lyric Postmodernisms,*[100] that the book is back from the printer. They're sending me my author's copies, so soon I will be able to cradle two babies in my arms.

You said that you were leaving a comment on Robert's blog, but I've seen no sign of such. Chop chop!

I just had the first day of my third round of chemo and have this neat new side-effect: I can't touch cold things without my fingers tingling and burning. And now even coolish room temperature liquids burn my throat. Fun fun. I wonder what's next.

Take good care. Is it cold in Oregon?

January 27, 2008
Alan to Reginald

I see that your baby [*Orpheus in the Bronx*] is born ! Well done. My copy should get here this week. I have been horribly overpressed with work and didn't want to give you a casual response to your last note. With luck, this week.

January 27, 2008
Alan to Reginald

I was looking back at your piece on Ann Lauterbach. I think there is a minor typo that might be worth fixing as it relates to locating the article:

Your blog says:

"Quotations from Reality," *Diacritics*, 26:3-4, Fall/Winter 1996. pp. 152, 153.

When I looked this up, it is called "Misquotations," not "Quotations."

I am trying to figure out if this paragraph is by Lauterbach or is a quotation from Stein. Can you enlighten me?

> "The aspiring young poet begins to write in such a way as to invite a certain critical attention, to 'fit' her work into one or another critical category. This is the main function of being identified with a group or school, to draw critical attention that individual poets, not affiliated with a movement or group, cannot easily attract. 'New York School' or

> 'Language Poetry' are given brand-name status, commodifying and homogenizing, so that critics (and poets) can make general identifications and totalizing critiques without having to actually contend with the specific differences among and between so-called members of the group. Those not so identified are left out, often understandably embittered or confused, as the idea of an individual iconoclastic poet gives way to collaborative and tribal identities. Thus the marginalized world of poetry begins to imitate other identity formulations which increasingly govern contemporary academic, cultural, and political life. Frightened by exclusionary clubs, the poet ceases to identify herself with the essential margin from which a vital critique must come."

Hope all is well. Snowing like hell here and several inches on the ground. We don't see this very often, and Eugene owns no snowplows except for the airport, which means that I might get tomorrow off, hope hope.

January 27, 2008
Reginald to Alan

Thanks for your note. I'm pretty sure that the article is called "Quotations from Reality," as I downloaded it from one of those online databases and that's the title is has there (I just checked). I sure hope so, since that same citation is my new book.

Damn! I just checked online and it is "Misquotations from Reality." I don't know how I messed that up, especially since I did download the article. Curse you for being right. Why couldn't you have seen this when there was still time for me to fix it in the book? Now the book has a glaring error in it and people will point at me and laugh, just like Nelson Muntz does on The Simpsons. Assholes. Mean, mean people.

The paragraph you asked about is by Lauterbach, not Stein (hence the references to the New York School and Language Poetry). If that's not clear, I'll have to go in and fix it. Along with the citation. Curses and drat.

Now I'm sulking...

I'm sorry to hear that it's been snowing so badly out there (I'm allergic to snow), but it will be good if it gets you the day off. It's been unseasonably cold down here—this past Monday morning when Robert was driving me to chemo there was ice on one of the roads (from spilled water). And it's gone down into the twenties a couple of nights, which is just wrong, wrong, wrong. Not to mention being wrong.

I've just started reading this book called *The Dirt on Clean*,[101] which is a history of Western practices and ideas of cleanliness—a topic close to my heart. I used to think that the Roman baths sounded really cool, but then I started thinking about all those people soaking in the same water, and now it sounds disgusting, like swimming in a public pool. Hopefully the grown Roman men didn't all pee in the water the way kids do. But still....

Take care, my friend, and here's to getting Monday off.

January 27, 2008
Alan to Reginald

Well, deep regrets from me for imperfecting your day. I think imperfecting should be a word. I just now noticed that citation; I'd never gone to the original before.

When I read your piece I assumed that the segment was Lauterbach because of the references. The only reason I was a little confused and felt the need for a recheck was that the very last segment in that series on your blog has a Stein citation, while the earlier ones don't have any citation at all. I think that part will be perfectly clear to anyone in the field.

So cheer up and don't get your colon in a twist !

PS no snow here in May, guaranteed !

January 27, 2008
Reginald to Alan

Well, I will try to untwist my colon and my knickers. I like that word "imperfecting." It's just about perfect. You should start a campaign to add it to the dictionary. I'd sign on.

I'm particularly embarrassed because I (mis)quote "Misquotations from Reality" not once but twice in my book. (Well, I guess I mis-cite; the quotations are accurate. But I liked the word play.) I was at least able to fix the citation on the blog, and I slightly rewrote the Stein quotation so it's more clear what it is.

Being right is one of the great pleasures of my life, so I hate to be deprived of it. :-)

I will hold you to your promise of no snow come May.

We're making fake lasagna (using squash ravioli) for dinner, taking off from an idea on Rachael Ray's 30-Minutes Meals (we love cooking shows and Food Network in general). She's annoyingly hyper-active and hyper-cutesy, but she has a lot of good ideas for stuff one would actually make, and could do so practically, even though almost none of it can be made in thirty minutes. Liar, liar! If I had a kitchen staff, I could make meals in thirty minutes too.

How do you feel about Kate Bush? I have a shrine to her in my heart. Also on my CD shelves and on my computers.

Take good care. I'm still rooting for a snow day for you.

January 27, 2008
Alan to Reginald

I've never heard of Kate Bush. I don't even know if that's a human or a kind of cotoneaster.

As for food, you and I are NOT destined for love: My kitchen is described by my friends as the place I store the pizza boxes. I never, ever think about food or pay any attention to it. I go to exactly the same restaurants (usually on the same day of the week) and order the same thing I had last time. Shopping for food is one of the great horrors of my life, and cooking, well, let us draw a kindly veil over what should not be seen.

I have a wonderful friend, Rich Hoyer, who is the great love of my life. I always thought that we'd be a perfect couple because he hates to write and loves to cook and garden. But he's still waiting for his Mr. Perfect (he's 38) and then there is the problem that he is Always Right.

I'd say 50-50 on the snow day. We had some melt, but not a lot, and should get more overnight.

January 28, 2008
Reginald to Alan

You don't like to cook and you don't know who Kate Bush is? Are you sure you're not straight? There's no reason to be ashamed if you are. Well, maybe as I look around at the world, there is...

Robert and I both love to cook, and we're both very good at it. We also work well together, and we've definitely made each other better cooks. We have two (small) bookcases of cookbooks, and we're always trying out new recipes, and of course improvising things. We rarely just follow a recipe straight.

Kate Bush is an Anglo-Irish singer/songwriter/producer whose first album, The Kick Inside, came out in 1978. Her best known songs are "Wuthering Heights" (in the voice of Cathy from the book) and "Running Up That Hill." My favorite albums of hers are The Dreaming and The Hounds of Love. You MUST look her up IMMEDIATELY. As in, RIGHT NOW. Listen to some songs on iTunes or something. She is utterly amazing.

Given that you know about all kinds of obscure music, I am shocked that you don't know of her, 'cause she's not that obscure.

As for Being Always Right, it's fine as long as I'm the one doing it. But I'm sorry that the potential love of your life is still waiting. Perhaps when he turns forty...

Kate Bush has a great song called "I'm Still Waiting."

Hope that you're getting the opportunity to enjoy a snow day.

January 28, 2008
Alan to Reginald

I will check her out This Very Day !

Does your cookbook shelf include the cookbook that goes with the Patrick O'Brian novels?[102] If not, I'll rectify that lacuna.

I kind of like the phrase "rectify that lacuna." Sounds like something done at night with a .22 down by the swamp. Strange splashings in the darkness, then silence and a whiff of pipe tobacco.

January 30, 2008
Alan to Reginald

I just ordered Hennessy's interview book.[103]

February 3, 2008
Alan to Reginald

Hey po dude, I have put a piece on my blog[104] that may or may not be a piece of shit. If you have time, I'd appreciate your look.

I'll have pieces in *Inside Higher Ed* next week and in the *Chronicle* the end of Feb. I am glorious (this month).

My local bookstore promises me your book on Tuesday....

February 3, 2008
Reginald to Alan

Hey other po dude,

I thought your piece was just terrific, and not just because you quote me and one of my favorite poets. It's funny, though, that you quote Kirsch in the context of talking about poetry and audience, since he was claiming on a panel I shared with him and two other much more intelligent people that poets don't care about an audience and only write for "posterity." I wrote about that in a post called "Readers Wanted," a few weeks ago.

Speaking of poets and their clubs, I just got back from the AWP conference, which to me at least was about the best example of such a club—everyone I met and talked with was really nice and very welcoming. It was only the second time I've ever gone, and I found it an exhilarating and overwhelming experience, especially since I pretty much don't talk to anyone except Robert when I'm at home.

Take good care, and keep the aspidistra flying. I think I already said that in an earlier post, but it always bears repeating.

February 3, 2008
Alan to Reginald

I'm glad you had a good meeting and that you think my piece is unshit. Kirsch didn't exactly say that poets need an audience, but he clearly is concerned that a lot of what is being written doesn't have enough escape velocity to get much past the poet's own teeth.

I just had a nice roll with a pleasant 46-year-old. This coming week I think I have a date with a 19-year-old blond musclehunk, aaaahhhh. If he shows up.

In DC for meetings the 10-12.

February 4, 2008
Alan to Reginald

I checked out Kate Bush. Interesting and original. Not likely to be a favorite of mine because my taste in female solo vocalists is somewhat limited. Thanks for suggesting that I check her out.

PS I cooked this evening. Just so you know.

February 7, 2008
Alan to Reginald

Your baby got here today. I ordered two and sent one over to Karen Ford so that she can be fully appreciative of your gloriousness.

February 7, 2008
Reginald to Alan

I'm glad that my baby was delivered safe and sound. I hope that you like it. Did you know that I actually had twins? I have a new poetry anthology, *Lyric Postmodernisms,* also just out. Amazon.com says it's out of stock, but that's because they haven't gotten it yet.

I wrote a post on the Poetry Foundation's Harriet blog (www.poetryfoundation.org/harriet) criticizing Charles Bernstein, among other things, and got *tons* of crazy people responding (including Chuck himself, twice). That I expected, though I never can anticipate just how insane people are, and how *many* insane people there are, because I'm not myself crazy.

But today I posted what I thought was a perfectly innocuous piece describing and defining "post-avant" poetry, a term which people bandy about all the time without saying what it is, and got a *torrent* of *insane, vicious* responses. What is up with these people? I've gone to AWP twice and met *hundreds* of people who were ALL nice, and yet almost *everyone* on these online forums is a nasty nutjob. Weird...

Why do you not like female vocalists? As a good card-carrying homo, female voices are by far my favorites, especially in classical music (and I always need the hook of a human voice in any kind of music to which I listen).

Did you know Roland Greene, who used to teach Renaissance poetry at UO? He was my teacher at Harvard, one of the few nice people there, and one of the few who actually liked and cared about poetry. I guess he's at Stanford now. I was thinking about writing him.

Take good care, my friend, and have a great weekend.

February 7, 2007
Alan to Reginald

I didn't know Greene. I used to be better connected to the UO, but many of the faculty I knew there have retired now.

I need to get serious about getting you a Portland gig. Portland is a natural place for you but the writing community there is somewhat hermetic and upper-crusty and I need to find the right crowbar to get it open. I do know Ursula Le Guin, and she knows everyone, so that be the best approach. If I had the time this spring I'd "produce" you myself in Portland, but I have too heavy a schedule.

I have to go to Washington DC Sunday for three days. After that I'll see who I can nag.

They'll put you in a nice B&B when you are here in May, but I'll drag you to my house for at least a brief visit so you can see your books on my shelf.

Female vocalists - there are some I like, Joan Baez, Connie Dover, Jessye Norman. I have always been a bad homo, though, in that I don't really care for a lot of them. Perhaps too much sameness in their songs, or the subject matter?

February 11 or 12, 2008
Alan to Reginald

I posted a comment to your latest blognote.

We have a solid offer for a reading in Portland on Sunday, May 18 at Powell's Books. This is the largest, most famous bookstore in the northwest and gets a huge gay clientele. Thus a good venue. They can't pay, but I can take care of your lodging there and any intercity travel. If this sounds good, you'll probably want an open-jaw air ticket (unless it is already reserved) into Eugene on Wednesday 14 and out of Portland either Sunday night (probably a bitch to get to Pensacola) or Monday morning 19th.

Are you up for it?

From Reginald Shepherd's blog, February 8, 2008
[http: / / reginaldshepherd.blogspot.com]

As I wrote in my earlier post, I will be posting the presentations that my panelists gave at the recent AWP conference. The presentations and the discussion after the panel made me question some of my positions about identity politics and poetry, so besides the general opportunity to hear some very smart and talented gay male poets discuss their reviews on the issue, it really stimulated and challenged my own thought, which I found invigorating.

Obeying the law of the alphabet, I will begin with Christopher Hennessy's untitled piece,[105] which started off the conversation on a high note. Once again, I encourage people to check out his blog,]Outside the Lines[, which approaches the question of the relationship of identity and creativity from many directions, and never with a sense that the answers are already known.

And now, here are Christopher's remarks:

> "Gay poet D.A. Powell has pointed out that queer poets are "doubly displaced," both gay and poet identifiers fixed outside the mainstream. It's a location poets like Powell fully inhabit and one I'd like to consider today. Powell said, "In the America of the 21st century, the poet is a displaced person. The queer poet, doubly displaced. (Thanks America, for nothing.) If there can be a useful consequence of living as a second-class citizen within this growing empire, it is that the range of possible subjects and forms expands also."
>
> Let's think about what the word "dis-placed" means:
>
> 1. To move or shift from the usual place or position, especially to force to leave a homeland: millions of refugees who were displaced by the war.
> 2. To take the place of; supplant.
> 3. To discharge from an office or position.
>
> Each of these definitions speaks to a loss of power of some

kind, but, on the contrary, for gay poets to be 'displaced' gives us a perspective and experiences that can, if we hone our craft, strengthen our work. But how 'displaced' are we?

When I started to think about what I would say today, I found I kept coming back to the idea of normal as a location, what it means to be 'normal…what it means to belong to the club, what it means to want to belong--and more importantly for gay artists, what it means to resist that, to proclaim difference rather than to mumble or even pretend normalcy. What do we create outside the borders of normal that we could not create, or would not create, if we were 'like everyone else'? The key to these questions lie in what aspects of our identity specifically keep us displaced, keep us from being normal. even at a time when homosexuality is losing its stigma. (A hint – it's the sex, of course. More on this later.) I think these questions are crucial to understanding where we go from here, as it were.

In order to have such a conversation, I've 'brought together' several of today['s] prominent and promising gay poets to join me in a sort of conversation."

David Trinidad: I guess it's always felt like the things I shouldn't or couldn't say are the things that I must say. For instance, putting one's sexual identity on the line felt like a risky thing to do in the 1970's; it also felt like a necessary thing to do. I think it's still risky, especially since gay poetry has become (since the late 80's) more coded, more conservative, as if it's trying to pass (I think of gay men getting married, raising babies) as straight. I always feel (whether it's true or not) that there's something unacceptable about my poems — they're too gay, too campy, too middle class. And that unacceptability is a big part of what makes my work (I hope) distinct.

CH: I think it's important David has noted the possibilities gay people now have, the relative safety we enjoy. Are gay poets trying to pass as straight? I'm not sure. We may no longer face persecution, but what about assimilation? I worry that being safe means the risk-taking, the boundary pushing, the edge-exploring will fade. Looking back, I'm thankful for the crucible of growing up gay because I think it's really affected me, in positive ways, as a writer.

Frank Bidart: To grow up gay in America is to know early that one's existence is fundamentally antithetical to the fictions desperately asserted by institutions that imagine their authority proceeds from God or nature. To know early that one's existence is fundamentally antithetical, period. That's a good start for a writer.

Joan Larkin, co-editor of the anthology *Gay and Lesbian Poetry in Our Time*: We are not just-like-straights-except-for one-thing. We are different because--often from an early age--many of us experience and see the world differently. Not separately, but distinctly--both the inside story and the outside story. It's often the gay writer who's taking risks for the entire culture. We're really good at that. From early childhood, many of use are faced with situations...we are forced to deal with....One of the daring things we do is write poems. Finding some way to tell the truth is part of staying sane. that's why our poems are often risky. And disturbing.

CH: In the past, we've had to create new metaphors, coded our language, disguised our desire, turned to myth and history and art as subjects in our poems when we wanted to talk about our differences--all strategies that refreshed the tradition, I think. And it's about more than that--it's about putting us in a position to see the world differently.

Mark Doty: Queerness invites us, every minute of our lives, to question our assumptions about what a man or a woman is, a mother or a father, a citizen; what is desire and what are the institutions we build around it, what does it mean to be desired, or the one doing the desiring? The position of questioning can keep an artist alive. I hope to never lose a liberating degree of distance from conventionality.

Alfred Corn: A contestatory stance: this is a good vantage point for an artist. We can see what the mainstream takes for granted, and we may call those axioms into question. Where there is no conflict or contestation, art is banal. Conflict comes to gay people ready-made, and we have to make use of it, in order not to be overwhelmed by it.

CH: I agree. Of course, it's not always easy, but I feel like if we have something unique to offer poetry, something that informs our individual voice, whether we want it to or not, we have a responsibility to the poems to utilize it, to understand it. (Understanding that 'it' is why I do my interviews!) But as society accepts us more and more, do we risk becoming 'normal'? I would argue not yet and perhaps never. Because let's be honest, a big part of what makes us different lies in sex, desire and our relationship to the body, since this is what most explicitly and most fundamentally makes us different. Sure, our love is no better or worse than heterosexual love, our sex and relationships no more or less messy, our right to love and lust no more valid. But because of a history of repression, oppression, and sublimation; because of seeing the body as a site of death and disease for decades after celebrating it as a place of transcendence; because physically we do things that are, shall we say, a creative use of our bodies, because of all of this, gay writers start in what turns out to be a frustrated place--a burning desire to speak about our love and eroticism but not knowing how to do so, and not being sure it's even safe to do so.

Alfred Corn again: When I contemplate the nature of sex between men, I find a counterpart in the art that gay men produce--a special searing intensity, the DMZ between pleasure and pain, synonyms for which might be "ravishment" or "rapture." Also, the ability to play both sides of the tandem, to understand both entering and being entered. Art has its analogues to these physical / psychological states.

CH: I think part of our work can be to analyze those 'analogues,' to understand how our desires get translated in our texts. I like what Alfred says but of course that is only one way our lives, unique and varied as they are and always have been, offer the work. How else might our experience affect our writing?

Carl Morse, co-editor of the *Gay and Lesbian Poetry in Our Time,* talking about the anthology's poems: Some of these experiences require recasting of the language--since no one has ever talked about them before--and these poets have done a lot of that. Gay and lesbian poetry refreshes the language. So much of this writing gets away from "polarity vocabularies."

CH: I'd like to think that our perspective on sex and desire gives us permission to expand the boundaries of poetry, to push what the lyric, for example, can accomplish. In the Michael Lassell and Elena Georgiou anthology *The World in Us,* the editors argue that our most important contribution is "the liberation of the libido."

J.D. McClatchy: Over the centuries, the homosexual temperament has seemed especially suited to engaging the themes of bafflement, secret joys, private perspectives, forbidden paradises, hypocritical conventions, and ecstatic occasions."

CH: I think it's important to note that McClatchy says "suited to engaging the themes,' not just 'suited to themes.' So for me, that means our talents lie not only in what we write but how we 'engage those themes', that is, how we convey our experiences onto the page. Well-known British poet and author of seminal texts on the history of gay poetry Gregory Woods argues that modern gay poets "have reflected the peculiarity of their social status by adapting correspondingly peculiar linguistic strategies." For example, in his A History of Gay Literature: The Male Tradition he explores how gay poets employ paradox. "Once one finds oneself to be para doxa, freed from the 'logic' of linguistic common sense and the 'natural' urges of the syntax we have been taught, all kinds of poetic dialects struggle to unfurl the tongue."

Our own **Brian Teare**: Though we often speak of experimentation exclusively in terms of what a poem does with syntax, the line, or the page, there are as many conventions about subject matte--and how we feel about certain subjects--to be tested. For instance, writing a good lyric poem about enjoying anal sex: that too is a resistance, a test of what poetry can do.

CH: I always think of Ginsberg in this respect. I read a review of his books once in which the critic said: "No other writer of his generation defended homosexual desire as a fit subject for poetry as effectively as Ginsberg" and doing so within "a vision of the world in which the asshole could be, rather than a source of shame, something deeply holy." I think that's an important function for a poet--turning a subject inside-out, upside down, from shameful to holy. But I wonder if today's poets are interested in that function, taking advantage of our ability to speak about those experiences that make us different?

Rick Barot: We're now in an amazing moment where artists can describe gay desire without having to camouflage it as something else. That desire can finally be an open subject matter, and this freedom has given us some recent writing that is scary, truthful, beautiful, and profoundly new.

CH: True as that may be, I think with it comes yet another problem, created, perhaps, in part, ironically, because of the levels to which Ginsberg pushed poetry. It's that a deference to difference often times means that those gay writers who embrace sexuality in their work, depict those elements of our lives explicitly, are forced to worry if we'll be seen as abandoning the poem's needs over a "personal" (of god forbid political!) desire to 'make a statement'. Or maybe that's just me. Of course, that doesn't stop us from writing the poems we must!

Our own **Aaron Smith**: I've felt like being overt/explicit in subject matter in "mainstream" poetry has been an uphill battle. It seems like since the late '80s early '90s there has been such a backlash against confessional poetry that anything narrative, seemingly personal, and/or sexual gets lumped under writing that is just for shock value. The writing is defined by that quality and not assessed for its craft, skill, and overall project. And so many writers are afraid to write personally for fear of being labeled a confessional poet.

CH: I personally hope we continue to embrace our differences as well as our similarities, no matter how post-gay we become. On that note, I'll give the last words to J.D. McClatchy and Rafael Campo. McClatchy tells us why the difficulties of our history give us urgency and necessity to express our differences.

J.D. McClatchy again: [Speaking about the poets in his anthology of gay love poetry] Because their desires have been deemed dangerous, and their lives made difficult, they place a unique value on true love.... Pleasure has been wrung from pain, illumination wrested from bitterness and fear, the moment of transcendence stolen from complacent hours.

CH: And Rafael Campo tells us how the triumph of our tradition gives us the permission and inspiration to write out our lives.

Rafael Campo: I realize that the gay literary aesthetic is one of hope, ultimately, where art is not simply a monument that displaces the truth of our existence, but rather is an insistence that we exist. At once edgily transgressive and universally humane, both painfully fractured and joyously restorative, queer writing is more than its artificial accomplishment in the eyes of critics; it is a document of persistence, an act of beauty, and the very breath and heartbeat of an imaginative and ultimately indomitable people.

February 8, 2008

Alan Contreras said...

Thanks, Reginald, for posting this interesting discussion. We look forward to your appearance at the University of Oregon in May.

I am a gay writer who writes poetry, though the great bulk of my writing is prose about higher education issues or ornithology. My poetry is very rarely about what I think of as "gay themes," yet I agree completely with the panelists who correctly perceive that gay writers by definition can't help but see society differently. I am IN society but I am not OF society.

I own every book of poems that J.D. McClatchy and you, Reginald, have published, and also all of Merrill, all of Carl Phillips and some works by Mark Doty. Many of the poems in these collections have a gay theme to them, but many do not.

I don't feel obligated to write about "gay things" because I am a gay person. It seems so cramped to limit oneself that way. Yet most of the panelists speak as though a gay poet has an obligation to focus on gay themes. Why?

Reginald Shepherd said...

Thanks for your comment, and I agree with your perspective. Christopher's presentation, the first I posted, is framed as a conversation, not a series of directives. I think of it as a conversation we are invited to join with our own voices and viewpoints.

I am no less a "gay" poet or a "black" poet when I am writing about house finches and pileated woodpeckers than when I am writing about late night cruising in Chicago (long in the past by now) or my childhood in the Bronx ghetto.

I do think that being or becoming gay has given me a different perspective, but that perspective informs everything I write and write about. Whatever I see, I see it a bit differently. But I see, and write about, a lot of things. I am utterly opposed to the idea that a gay writer should write in a certain way or on certain topics.

I've just posted another piece from the panel, by the wonderful poet (and one of my closest friends) Brad Richard, which goes very far in questioning (even exploding) the whole notion of "gay poetry." I think that you'll find it of interest.

February 12, 2008
Reginald to Alan

That would be fabulous if I could do a reading at Powell's, which I know quite well--there are a couple in Chicago I used to patronize all the time, and I've mail ordered from them several times since moving out of the city.

But if my UO reading is on May 15, that would be a *long* trip, really too long for me. Is there a way to push the UO reading closer to the Powell's reading? Let me know what's possible. I'd hate to miss this great opportunity, but I don't think I could handle that long a trip, especially in my current delicate condition.

peace and poetry, Reginald

[*followup message the same day*] Oh, I forgot to mention that I posted a comment in response to your comment. I don't remember exactly what I said, but it was good, and it addressed your concerns, with which I totally concur. "Give me land, give land, give me country that I love—don't fence me in."

Also, I'm very proud of you for actually making your own dinner. You might turn out to be a homosexual yet. We'll have to see how you pass the other tests...

Februrary 11 or 12, 2008
Alan to Reginald

I got on ABE this evening and ordered a copy of the Samuel Delany book you mentioned in your intro.[106] There were only 9 copies available in the US !

I am a big sci-fi fan and the only book-length fiction I have done (unpublished so far) has been that kind. That's what I'll do more of when I retire.

I have never read ANY Adorno. What should I start with?

February 12, 2008
Reginald to Alan

What Delany book did I mention in what intro? I've been writing a lot of stuff lately and I totally can't keep track of anything. They're all good—he's one of my favorite writers.

When I was a kid pretty much the only stuff I read was sci-fi, history, and natural history. I don't reach much of it now, but I love Delany, Joanna Russ, Gwyneth Jones, Elizabeth Hand, and Dan Simmons.

God I adore Adorno, but he ain't easy. He's easier than people think he is, though, if they just pay attention. I think that *Aesthetic Theory*[107] is his best book, though the only currently available translation, from the University of Minnesota Press, is designed to be as difficult to read as possible (no section breaks, and Greek words aren't even transliterated, for example). There's an earlier, out of print translation from Routledge that's much more readable. It can be found online. His two volume collection of essays, *Notes to Literature*,[108] is also good, and contains my favorite single piece of his, "Lyric Poetry and Society."

Take good care, my friend.

February 13, 2008
Alan to Reginald

Check out my latest in Inside Higher Ed.[109]

February 13, 2008
Reginald to Alan

Hey Alan,

Thanks for the shout-out in your article; I really appreciate the mention. I was reading your comments, and it's interesting to see that the problem of people running off at the keyboard without bothering to read or think about what they're criticizing isn't limited to poetry blogs. It makes me feel a bit better, actually.

By the way, as I wrote earlier, I posted a response to your comment on one of my gay boy poetry posts[110] that I hope should address your concerns. The whole thing was meant to be a conversation, not a sermon on the mount of how to be a good gay writer, because I am SO not into that. Brad Richard's piece, which is the next one I posted, questions the whole concept of being a "gay writer." Check it out.

peace and poetry (especially, lord, some peace), Reginald

February 13 or 14, 2008
Alan to Reginald

I have a very special book to send you, ha ha !

I am also purging my shelves of duplicate copies of some things, do you want any of:

Recitative, Selected Prose of James Merrill

The Estate of Poetry, Edwin Muir

The Struggle of the Modern, Stephen Spender (this, which I had never heard of, is way better than his poetry)

February 14, 2008
Reginald to Alan

Hey handsome,

I love very special books. Does it have naked guys in it? I like naked guys too.

I would love to have copies of all the books that you mentioned. (I actually read *The Estate of Poetry*[111] in college. It's good stuff.) That's incredibly generous of you. There are two Stephen Spender poems I love: "I Think Continually of Those Who Are Truly Great" ('cause, you know, I do, and even aspire to join them) and "Polar Exploration." There's also a really gay poem in his first book that I really like; I don't remember the title (it was untititled, I think) and I don't think he ever reprinted it.

People are still picking on me online, like the self-righteous blowhard Joshua Clover, but I'm trying to say that it's okay, because part of becoming a public figure is that there's this effigy (or several) of you floating out there that has your name and maybe even your face, but has nothing to do with you at all. That's what I try to tell myself.

It's almost time to for bed. Happy Valentine's Day.

February 14 or 15, 2008
Alan to Reginald

Joshua Clover, hmm. I have one of his books. Quite impressed with himself but an interesting poet. One of the "modern" poets whose work I sometimes gaze upon.

I get picked on online all the time. The diploma mill owners all over the world call me The Fat Homo and trash my reputation. That is because I am GLORIOUS. And so are y'all.

February 15, 2008
Reginald to Alan

I have known Joshua on and off for over fifteen years, and have been close with a number of his (former) friends. He is rude, egotistical, self-righteous, condescending, superior-acting, and just generally an ass. He's also rich and has a tenured job, which makes his pseudo-leftist posturing especially hard to take (what has he transgressed or negated lately, besides the bounds of civil debate and reasoned argument?).

On the other hand, I thought *Madonna Anno Domini* [112] was a terrific book, and I've liked a lot his other work. (I invited him to be in my Iowa *Anthology of New American Poetries*, but he refused because it was insufficiently "transgressive" and "subversive," whatever that's supposed to mean.) His most recent book, *The Totality for Kids*, seems too much a set of notes to theory we've already read, thank you very much, though there are some good poems there.

He strikes me as someone with real talent who has consciously chosen to squander it, not to mention to waste his genuine intelligence on some weird nihilistic version of leftism that completely excludes the real world and real people. But then, so much academic pseudo-leftism does—these people know nothing about reality, and then attack me, for example, as Clover has done on more than one occasion, for being reactionary. Really, if I [could] arrange for him to be hit by a Mack truck while riding around on his skateboard, I would.

I need to get used to the online bullies. I got over them in high school, I should get over them now. Pretty fucking rude and homophobic, these online assholes who attack you. Do people ever think about what they're writing, if not before they write it at least before they post it? It's as if none of the rules of normal human discourse apply online. Freaky and disturbing.

Glory, glory, glory. That's us. They're just jealous. (I really think they are. A lot of people resent anyone who's done anything with himself besides whine and complain--which I do.)

Time for breakfast. Take care, my friend, and thanks in advance for the books.

peace and poetry and to hell with the haters, Reginald

February 15, 2008
Alan to Reginald

I think your analysis of Clover is right on. I have read a couple of interview pieces with him over the years and he reminds me a lot of the kind of gasping "liberals" who constitute much of the population of south Eugene. Latté revolutionaries.

One of your very great strengths is that you can separate the bitch from the litter (jeez I like that phrase) and look at the poet's work as work, decoupled (sometimes needs a pry-bar and a gallon of WD-40) from their personality. That is something very uncommon, if you look around in our culture.

More later.

February 15, 2008
Alan to Reginald

You can't play for safety and make art. See Clinton, Hillary.

February 17, 2008
Reginald to Alan

Thanks for the kind words. I do try to read the work and the person separately. If we couldn't do that, there's a lot of work (Ezra Pound the actual fascist, for example) that we just couldn't read. Even Chuck Marx said that Balzac's reactionary views didn't impede the insights of his work.

I asked Clover to be in my first anthology, but it was insufficiently transgressive for him. I hated him then, too, but I thought his work belonged. And I listed him among the "post-avant" poets in my Poetry Foundation post, which has now been mentioned twice on the *Chronicle of Higher Education* web site. They seemed rather bemused by all the infighting, but they did note that I had pointed it out as an issue. I'm revising and expanding that piece for my own blog, where at least I will get to delete comments that tick me off.

I'm so loving that phrase separating the bitch from the litter. The litter is often pretty damned filthy indeed.

My new New Year's resolution: not to argue with idiots and assholes. It'll be hard, but I'm gonna try, if only for the sake of my own mental health.

Since you're not into female voices (some homo, you), I won't even mention Dusty Springfield. But she will always be a goddess of popular music. And she sang a song about how sex in the morning gets the day off right. Please note my clever pun.

February 17, 2008
Alan to Reginald

My pun detector indeed located your pun and you are hereby awarded one pun-credit. There must be a word for that.

I always found James Merrill's utter detachment from the norms of daily life somewhat disconcerting (he is said to have never voted or read a newspaper), but he remains one of my favorite poets.[113]

You do a good job of focusing on the work rather than the worker. It isn't always easy. There is an odd guy in Eugene who is known mainly for what I will delicately call his attitude toward women, punctuated by the weird yard sculptures he erected to, er, honor a woman who lives on his block. Years ago (1979) I remember him as the dude who would lumber into the 7-11 where I was on night shift, buy a carton of cottage cheese, stand outside the store and eat it by dipping his hand into it. But he was also the finest woodcarver I have ever known; his whales were found all over town. Not sure if he does them any more.

February 17, 2008
Alan to Reginald

Orpheus is magnificent ! Your gloriousness has once again been set in gold.

One thing that particularly stuck with me is the idea that the self is created (I am certainly a work in progress). I have always wondered why people allow Them to decide who we are, instead of deciding that for ourselves. Easier?

The mainstream: broad, sluggish and muddy. No shit.

The Stevens discussion was really good and may yet move me to read more Stevens. I have his collected[114] but have read very little. No excuse, just the way things have been.

February 17, 2008
Reginald to Alan

Ah, Alan, you are a true angel. Just like the song says, you're as sweet as Tupelo honey, just like honey from the bees. I really am glad that you like that book. Honestly, I'm proud of it. I should be—I worked on it for at least four years, longer, I think.

I've always thought of myself as a work in progress. I certainly hope so, 'cause there's definitely room for improvement.

Anything that encourages people to read more Wallace Stevens is a good thing in my book. He's a necessary angel of the first degree.

February 23, 2008
Alan to Reginald

My copy of Delany's *The Jewel-Hinged Jaw* got here today and I have started into it. What a journey this will be. I can definitely see what you like about him.

February 23, 2008
Reginald to Alan

The *Jewel-Hinged Jaw* was, like, my bible in high school. I learned so much about writing and reading from it. It's utterly out of print, and hard to find used. How did you come across it? He has a new book about writing, called, reasonably enough, *About Writing,*[115] which is just brilliant. If I were still teaching, I would assign it to all of my students.

Did I tell you that when I saw my oncologist last week, during my fourth round of chemo, he said that the cancer markers in my blood have gone down from eleven to three? I don't know exactly what that means, but he's ordered a CAT scan for after my next round of chemo, and if the liver tumors have shrunk enough, they may be able to operate to remove them. It's good news, but I don't want to get my hopes up.

I also got a bill for $1100 for one month of chemo (I *hope* it was for the whole month). Plus the hospital where I had my lithotripsy in September to break up my kidney stones now says that I owe them $700, after insurance, even though I never got a bill. The woman I spoke to was like, "Do you want to set up a payment plan?" and I was like "I'd rather see an actual bill first." Don't you like the verb "to be like"?

It's getting late and I need to start getting ready for bed--my little rituals take a while.

Good night, sweet prince.

February 23, 2008
Alan to Reginald

Very good news about your glorious colon. Staying alive is expensive. With luck you will win lots of awards in the year ahead.

I ordered *Jewel-hinged Jaw* off ABE based on the mention you made of it in the intro to Orpheus. There are VERY few copies available out there and they are not cheap. I'm going to fish around the larger used bookstores in Oregon as time permits and see if I can find another one.

I'll order the new one. *Jaw* is wonderful but a little dated on the actualities of the s-f world. The great bulk of my unpublished output is sci-fi novels, and that is how I plan to spend my energy after I retire from state service in three years. Cleaning up and trying to publish the ones that exist, finishing two that are languishing half-cooked, and pursuing new ideas.

February 24, 2008
Alan to Reginald

Reading Delany's detailed comment on Ursula Le Guin's *The Dispossessed,*[116] I was astonished to come across a quote from a speech of hers to a lit club here in Eugene. She's from Oregon, of course—in fact she and I are acquainted slightly from many years at the same book signing event in Portland—but it was a strange thing to come across. She's not a bad poet and is something of a birder, too.

February 26, 2008
Reginald to Alan

I just got the big box of books you sent me. THANK YOU so much! It was way more than I was expecting. The Spender book should be interesting; I think I read some other prose book of his a long time ago. I read *The Estate of Poetry* in college and thought it very good, but I don't remember anything specific about it.

Have you ever read *Camp Concentration* by Thomas M. Disch?[117] Delany writes about it at length in *The Jewel-Hinged Jaw,* which is what made me read it. But I don't remember much about it (I was in high school), though I remember liking it.

Delany's essay collection *Longer Views,*[118] which Wesleyan University Press published, has a lot of stuff about sci-fi, which is what he calls a "paraliterary" genre.

March 3 (?), 2008
Alan to Reginald

Hey homotextual, take care of yourself. I had the flu-slime and it knocked me onto my keister[119] for a week. If that's what you have, just plan for a week of tired butt-dragging and don't push it.

I have Brenda Hillman's *Death Tractates,*[120] do you know that collection? I am woefully ignorant of Ashbery - no excuses, just haven't read more than a couple of items. I have *Double Dream of Spring*[121] and that's it. Is he worth more energy? My attempts at Jorie Graham have foundered so far. But that is also true of Joyce's *Ulysses*.

I gave Karen Ford at UO a copy of *Orpheus* in order that she might be more fully exposed to your glory, and she immediately talked about using something from it in a class she is teaching. I'm not sure what got her all excited.

March 3 (?) 2008
Alan to Reginald

Just read your latest. Much to ponder. My taste in poets runs to more traditional sounds, though I stick my toes into modern waters from time to time.

Note error in citations:

Ross, Andrew. *The Rest Is Noise: Listening to the Twentieth Century*. New York: Farrar Straus Giroux, 2007.

Should be Ross, Alex. You have it right in main text.

March 3, 2008
Reginald to Alan

Thanks for your note. I'm glad that you like the post, even if the poetry I'm writing about isn't to your taste. I like a wide range of things. I hate a wide range of things too. Often they overlap. Basically, I like good things and I hate things that suck (in the bad way).

Thanks for pointing out the mis-citation. Andrew Ross is a big time cultural theorist (though his first book was about T.S. Eliot) whom I used to read a lot. (He was interviewed in GQ a million years ago or so about the semiotics of fashion. I want that gig, but cultural studies is pretty much over, unless you're a TV commentator on pop princesses. I could do that.) At least this mistake I can fix, unlike the Lauterbach mis-citation in *Orpheus in the Bronx*. And today I discovered a typo in the book, despite my and Michigan's copy-editors having gone over it diligently. Drat.

Take care, my friend. I feel like crap (a nasty cold/flu that won't go away), and tomorrow I'm starting my fifth round of chemo, so I have a fun week to look forward to. Yeesh.

I like interjections. Particularly silly ones.

March 6, 2008
Reginald to Alan

Hey Sunshine,
I am sick as a dog, or sicker, thanks to my latest round of chemo, but I wanted to thank you for the terribly nice things you wrote about me to my publicist at Pitt (who is an incredibly nice and together person). And thanks again for sponsoring me.

Thanks also, again, for the books. I was reading the crazed sea-captain cookbook today; it's pretty cool, though you'll never catch me eating rat, whatever euphemism you choose to use, with or without onion sauce. I liked the blurb on the back of Robert McDowell's book[122] that slagged off "ornate pretentiousness," since I love ornate pretentiousness. :-) And Mr. Merrill really didn't write much prose, did he? *Recitative*[123] is almost all interviews. Well, I guess he did write a novel. I even read it, years and years ago. I recall nothing about it, though, but I think I liked it.

March 6, 2008
Alan to Reginald

Good to hear your voice, as it were.

Reading your latest blog, and also the latest Oregon poetry society newsletter, I find the same word: emerging. I find myself wondering just what constitutes an emerging poet. Some (you, Merrill, Phillips, Ashbery come to mind) were clearly the Full Meal Deal from the very beginning. There wasn't any real question of qualitative status. Others start out as what you might call journeyman poets and build a reputation slowly over time.

What constitutes emergence? Quality, quantity, recognition by some particular high court of words?

I may blog on this question at some point. Any thoughts?

PS, we don't say rat, we say "miller" to make them taste better.[124] And what better revenge than a good stir-fry (remove tail and feet)? !!!!

Probably early April, 2008
Alan to Reginald

Congrats on your Guggenheim, though I really don't know what it entails. Stacks of swag and some public notice, I hope.

See you soon.

> "Every time I hear a political speech or I read those of our leaders, I am horrified at having, for years, heard nothing which sounded human. It is always the same words telling the same lies. And the fact that men accept this, that the people's anger has not destroyed these hollow clowns, strikes me as proof that men attribute no importance to the way they are governed; that they gamble—yes, gamble—with a whole part of their life and their so-called 'vital interests'." [125] --Albert Camus, 1937

April 3, 2008
Reginald to Alan

The Guggenheim involves lots of prestige and a nice chunk of money—I don't know exactly how much, but they say that their fellowships "average" $39,000, which is several years' income for me. Most of that will go to my ever-mounting medical bills, especially now that my COBRA group coverage is running out and I'm switching to a much more expensive individual policy.

"Swag" is a funny word. Where does it come from? Is it because one swaggers when one's rich? I see Bill Gates doing that all the time. Bastard...

Take good care, and see you soon.

[*Shepherd had a serious medical relapse shortly after and had to cancel his appearance in Oregon*]

June 9, 2008
Alan to Reginald

Greetings. I trust that you remain undead.

I am taking a week off to avoid my duties and get some birding, reading and writing done. So far not very productive, but I just posted a little promo blurb for *Orpheus* on my blog, which must be read by, oh, ten people monthly. Hope the book is doing well.

And are you doing well? Send me a note when you can.

Parini's *Why Poetry Matters* [126] is pretty good. I wasn't sure what to expect, since I don't always like his essays.

I have attached a photo of where I am, my retreat locale for 38 years now,[127] and a pic of me being productive.

Reginald Shepherd's Orpheus

I am pleased to recommend the following:

Orpheus in the Bronx Essays on Identity, Politics and the Freedom of Poetry, by Reginald Shepherd

This is Shepherd's first full-length collection of essays related to poetry and the creative arts, and it brings his usual brilliance and clarity to bear on a wide variety of issues:

> "A poem has never oppressed anyone, though I was once on a panel at a gay writers' conference with a black lesbian performance poet who implied that literacy was oppressive to black people, which certainly would have been news to the slaveowners who tried to keep their property from learning to read."

This is the kind of blow-off-the-cultural-cobwebs-with-a-jet-turbine writing that is rare in most books and common in *Orpheus*. Shepherd, whose identity is made the old-fashioned way, with original work, has a great deal to say about identity poetry based on collective defense perimeters rather than true individuality. He also discusses the nature of the urban experience and its connection to poetry, why he has chosen to write and other topics of interest to anyone who writes or reads poetry.

The book also contains exceptionally perceptive commentary on the work of Alvin Feinman, Genet, Wallace Stevens, Linda Gregg, Samuel R. Delany, Aaron Shurin, Donald Britton, Tim Dlugos, D. A. Powell and Jorie Graham. Graham is a poet whose work I have always had trouble appreciating: thanks to Shepherd, I can approach her work from a new angle that may shed more light than the old ones.

Shepherd also provides a useful mirror to what really happens in today's writing, for example:

> "...much mainstream American poetry (and there is indeed a mainstream, broad, sluggish and muddy) seems never to have heard of modernism (or even, in too many cases, of Keats), retailing equally aimless examples of therapeutic self-exploration or convenient epiphanies in prosaic anecdotes not interesting or shapely enough to be short stories: what has been called the 'I look out the window and I am important (or sensitive)' school."

Buy it. Read it.

June 10-11, 2008[128]
Reginald to Alan

I am indeed still among the not-dead, though very much among the walking wounded (also a wonderful song by Everything But the Girl), with fever, fatigue, nausea and vomiting, a deep cough, and general cruddiness. I'd been taken off the IV antibiotics, but now have been put back on them, because I clearly need them. They're definitely helping. And Robert is, as usual, a whole hierarchy of angels. He really takes care of me. I tell him that I won't want to be a burden to him (I can't do much for myself), and he says I'm not, but it's all definitely stressful for him as well.

Thanks for your kind words about *Orpheus in the Bronx* on your blog, which are much appreciated, and which were also pointed out to me by someone else. Just so you'll know that people do read your blog.

I am going to sign off now and get ready for bed, which I should have already started—my night time rituals always take longer than I think they will. Everything I do takes longer than I think it will.

Take good care, my friend, and I hope to finally meet you next year.

peace and poetry, Reginald

I just remembered that the "someone" who pointed me toward your blog entry on *Orpheus* was Samuel R. Delany. Now you're playing with the big boys.

June 10-11, 2008
Alan to Reginald

Oh my. Delany. What does one say? I suddenly remember what a very sloppy writer I often am. It is so very good to hear your voice. More later.

Late June, 2008
Alan to Reginald

The Olympic trials are underway here, and the hot weather has brought out SKIN in profusion, yahoooooo ! I hope that you are doing well.

Adam Kirsch's new collection *Invasions*[129] has some good poems in it. I like his poetry better than his criticism.

I sent you a few books maybe a month or six weeks back. Did they get there? I know you probably have a pile of stuff.

Looks like I'll be able to escape the office for FOUR WEEKS this fall, sneaking off to the desert and spending mornings birding, afternoons doing work for my office via the field station's wifi tower and evenings working on my own writing. Ahhhhh....

If it were not for the patterns in life, improvisations would not be noticed.

June 27, 2008
Reginald to Alan

Well, I'm sure it's nice for you to be surrounded by nice human scenery. I was just telling my friend Merav this afternoon that I really want to live somewhere with a) smart people, b) attractive people, and c) gay boys. Pensacola doesn't really cut it on any of those counts.

I did indeed get the package you sent me, including the copy of your book, but it was during my more-than-a-month-long sojourn in the hospital (I'm sure you know about that--if not, I'll be happy to share my near-death experience with you).

I am slowly and fairly steadily recovering, though with frequent setbacks. The nausea and fatigue caused by the daily IV antibiotic infusions which are supposed to help me get better are not fun.

I've decided that I'm getting bored with "avant-garde"/"experimental" poetry. I like poems that have something to say, that are about something. But they have to be beautiful, which rules out most such poems. Or most poems period. But lately I can't concentrate to read poetry at all, so at the moment it's a moot point.

I got a royalty check from Michigan for *Orpheus in the Bronx*. You like me, you really like me!

It's getting late and I need to go to bed (see above re: fatigue). Take good care, my friend, and enjoy your four weeks of vacation.

June 28 2008
Alan to Reginald

No, Pensacola is not the pulsing heart of culture or skin. The job market being weird and your partner having a Real Job must be somewhat constricting.

Congrats on the royalty payment. There is something very comforting about the phrase "check enclosed." Mine is due from Oregon State U Press in a few weeks. It will be maybe $75 or so, since my bird books have all been out for a while, but hey, that's a nice offset to gas prices.

More later.

August 7, 2008
Alan to Reginald

Hey favorite fruit, good to see you posting. How is your much-perforated person these days?

Have you reconnected with UO regarding a visit this year? The airfare is good through early May 09. I'll be out of town Sep 13-Oct 10 and hope to see you sometime after that.

August 8, 2008
Reginald to Alan

Hey Alan, Thanks for your note and good wishes. I just got out of a three-week stint in the hospital for surgery to fix an abdominal fistula (I was leaking fecal matter from my colon to a hole in my abdomen—fun fun). Since then I've been going to my doctor's office every morning for two and a half hours to do medication infusions, but now they say I can do the infusions at home (as I'm sure I always could have), which will make my life *much* better.

What with this whole new set of required recovery, something in the spring sounds like it would make the most sense, if you let Karen Ford. I really am determined to get out there one of these years...

Take care, mein freund, and enjoy your vacation, if that is indeed what it is.

September 1, 2008
Alan to Reginald

Hey R. I hope the hurricane goes where you are not.

Just saw this [Willamette Univ.] job announcement. Perhaps you or someone you know would be interested. They might take an MFA with a good record.

1. African American Literature
2. Ethnic American Literature
3. Poetry & Creative Writing

Three positions are available, one in each area of interest listed. Publications in the field are required & for Poetry & Creative writing a PhD in literature, emphasizing poetry, preferably from the 19th century to present is required.

Review begins Nov. 7, 2008 for all positions. Interviews will be conducted at the MLA in San Francisco between Dec. 27 and Dec. 30, 2008.

Conclusion

Shepherd died on September 10, 2008. I did not realize at the time of my September 1 message that he was in the final stages of his disease. We never met. I feel the absence of that meeting as a great weight. For some reason I kept almost every e-mail we sent back and forth, as though I had a premonition. I have never done this with another correspondent. Seldom have I encountered such a pure, shining intelligence. Seldom, too, a person less ready to depart, which makes his loss seem unjust.

Reginald Shepherd was one of the nation's most interesting poets and best writers about poetry and the experience of creating it. A graduate of the University of Iowa and Brown University, his works include *Some are Drowning* (1994); *Angel, Interrupted* (1996); *Wrong* (1999); *Otherhood* (2003); *Fata Morgana* (2007); *Orpheus in the Bronx* (2007, Michigan), *A Martian Muse* (2010, Michigan) and *Red Clay Weather* (2011); all from Pittsburgh except as noted.

Reginald once sent me an e-mail addressed to "Sunshine" and concluded with "Goodnight, sweet prince," but even that one ended with his unique good-bye, so with his words I must say my good-bye: "peace and poetry" forever, my unmet friend.

Note: Pittsburgh also issued *The Selected Shepherd* (Jericho Brown, ed.), April 2024.

Notes

1 In this book I use the word "gay" as a generic for sexualities outside the hetero norm; likewise the word "lesbian" is used as a female generic. In some cases other words such as "queer" or "trans" are used when they seem necessary.

2 Lebowitz, Fran. "The Voice: Fran Lebowitz." *Interview Magazine*, March 11, 2016. Quote sourced from Wikipedia, April 5, 2024.

3 Hennessy, Christopher. *Outside the Lines: talking with contemporary gay poets* (Michigan, 2005).

4 Shepherd, Reginald. *Orpheus in the Bronx*, p. 52 (Michigan, 2007).

5 Chamberlain, Lesley. *Rilke: The Last Inward Man* p. 87 (Pushkin, 2022).

6 Rilke, Rainer Maria, in a letter to his wife Clara; see Chamberlain, *Rilke: The Last Inward Man.*

7 See interview with Carl Phillips, *Sewanee Review*, Fall 2022.

8 MacDonald, Dwight. *Masscult and Midcult*, p. 17. New York Review Books (2011). This essay is reprinted from versions that appeared in 1953 and earlier articles.

9 Ross, Alex. The Fate of the Critic in the Clickbait Age, *The New Yorker*, March 13, 2017.

10 Vargas Llosa, Mario. *Notes on the Death of Culture*, p. 21. Farrar, Straus, Giroux (2012).

11 Kennedy, Angus. *Being Cultured*, p. 78. Societas (2014).

12 Ibid. at p. 101.

13 Extracted from *The Unforgivable* by Cristina Campo (1923-1977), translated from the Italian by Alex Andriesse. This brilliant collection became available in English in 2024 via New York Review Books. The bracketed bit is mine.

14 Roberts, Stephen. *Deep Song: The Life and Work of Federico Garcia Lorca* (Reaktion, 2020).

15 Valis, Noel. *Lorca After Life* (Yale, 2022).

16 Backhouse, Bebe. *More Than These Bones* (Magawala, 2023). The author changed his surname to Backhouse-Oliver to reflect his marriage to Jeremy Oliver shortly after the book was published. The publisher is based in Broome, Western Australia and specializes in books by or about the aboriginal peoples of the Australian continent.

17 *Adam in the Garden*, A.E. Hines (Charlotte Lit Press, 2024). See also his first collection *Any Dumb Animal* (Main Street Rag Publishing, Charlotte, 2021).

18 Duberman, Martin. 2014. *Hold Tight Gently: Michael Callen, Essex Hemphill and the Battlefield of AIDS* (The New Press, 2014).

19 Hemphill, Essex. 1992. *Ceremonies* (Penguin [Plume]).

---

20 This can be done, with a certain determination. I have been involved in reviving the work of Ada Hastings Hedges and Ernest G. Moll.

21 *In Search of Silence: The Journals of Samuel R. Delany, Volume 1, 1957-1969*, edited by Kenneth R. James, Wesleyan University Press.

22 Romm, James. *The Sacred Band* (Scribner, 2021)

23 Luczak, Raymond. *Lovejets: Queer Male Poets on 200 years of Walt Whitman.* (Squares and Rebels, Minneapolis, 2019).

24 Berg, James J. and Chris Freeman, Editors. *Isherwood in Transit* (Minnesota, 2020).

25 Roffman, Karen. *The Songs We Know Best: John Ashbery's Early Life* (FSG, 2017).

26 Cotton, Jess. *Critical Lives: John Ashbery* (Reaktion, 2023)

27 See, Sam and others. *Queer Natures, Queer Mythologies* (Fordham, 2020).

28 Gilbert, Sandra. *Adrienne Rich, Essential Essays: Culture, Politics, and the Art of Poetry* (Norton, 2018).

29 Le Guin, Ursula, translator and editor. *Selected Poems of Gabriela Mistral* (New Mexico, 2003, 2011).

30 Moore, Darnell. *No Ashes in the Fire: Coming of Age Black and Free in America* (Nation, 2018).

31 Lauritsen, John, *Don Leon and Leon to Annabella* (Pagan, 2017)

32 Noted in an essay on Merrill, "Braving the Elements," by J.D. McClatchy, *The New Yorker*, March 27, 1995, reprinted in *Twenty Questions* (Columbia, 1998).

33 See Fricke's *Reflections of a Rock Lobster* (Alyson, 1981) for his own narrative of the prom case, which eventually went to court.

34 Klawitter, George. *Andrew Marvell, Sexual Orientation and Seventeenth-Century Poetry* (Fairleigh Dickinson University Press).

35 Phillips, Carl. *The Tether* (FSG, 2002)

36 Antonia, Nina, Editor. *Incurable: The Haunted Writings of Lionel Johnson, the Decadent Era's Dark Angel* (Strange Attractor, 2019).

37 "Loren's Song," included in the 2018 collection *In the Time of the Queen.*

38 See the exchange of emails in *A Conversation with Reginald Shepherd* in this volume.

39 Shepherd died shortly after this piece was written. See "A Conversation with Reginald Shepherd," in this volume.

40 http://reginaldshepherd.blogspot.com/

41 The term "commodity" was also applied to certain kinds of modern poetry by Alaska's poet laureate John Haines in his essay "The Young American Poets," published in the fall, 1969 issue of *kayak* and reprinted in his book *Living Off the Country: Essays on Poetry and Place* (Michigan, 1981). I did not realize this until preparing this collection in 2024.

---

42 Camus, Albert. *Notebooks 1942-1951*, p. 201. Trans. Justin O'Brien. Paragon (1991).

43 The 2024 introduction has been slightly revised and updated from the 2013 original.

44 *The Selected Shepherd.* Jericho Brown, editor (Pittsburgh, 2024)

45 Patrick O'Brian places this perfect statement on the tongue of Maturin in the novel *The Nutmeg of Consolation*, p. 258.

46 Shepherd, Reginald. *Orpheus in the Bronx* (Michigan, 2007).

47 *Some are Drowning*, 1994; *Angel, Interrupted*, 1996; *Wrong*, 1999; *Otherhood*, 2003; *Fata Morgana*, 2007; *Red Clay Weather*, 2011; all from Pittsburgh.

48 *See* Coues, Elliott in *Behind the Veil* (1880), cited in *Elliott Coues: Naturalist and Frontier Historian*, p. 429. Paul R. Cutright and Michael J. Brodhead, 1981. Illinois.

49 *A Martian Muse* (Michigan, 2010).

50 The full statement, from Vol. 2 of the *Journals of André Gide*, Justin O'Brien, trans. (1948), p. 306 is "The reasons that impel me to write are multiple, and the most important ones, it seems to me, are the most secret. Perhaps this one above all: to have something secure against death—and this is what makes me, in my writings, seek among all other qualities those upon which time has the least grasp and by which they escape all passing fads."

51 The prize is currently inactive.

52 I recommend Jim and Jean's or Glenn Yarbrough's recordings of "Crucifixion" because the best Phil Ochs performance (a live one) is hard to find and is, as of this writing, not available online. The original studio recording by Ochs features shockingly ill-conceived orchestration.

53 Mallett, Robert ed. *Self-Portraits: The Gide-Valéry Letters*, 1890-1942, abridged and translated by June Guicharnaud, Chicago, 1966). To give an idea of the changing role of letters as a part of daily life for literary people, consider that full-length collections have been published not only of Gide-Valéry, but of Gide-Edmund Gosse, Gide-Dorothy Bussy, Gide-Paul Claudel, Gide-Arnold Bennett and something similar for Gide-Oscar Wilde. To be sure, Gide was an extraordinarily productive letter-writer who lived to write, but one cannot imagine anything remotely close to his output of letters today.

54 Faggen, Robert ed. *Striving Towards Being: the Letters of Thomas Merton and Czeslaw Milosz* (FSG, 1996).

55 Biddle, Arthur, ed. *When Prophecy Still Had a Voice: the Letters of Thomas Merton and Robert Lax*. (Kentucky, 2001).

56 Gershator, David ed. and translator. *Federico Garcia Lorca, Selected Letters.* (New Directions, 1983).

57 Howe, M. A. DeWolfe ed. *John Jay Chapman and his Letters* (Houghton Mifflin, 1937).

58 Rorem, Ned. *Wings of Friendship, Selected Letters, 1944-2003* (Shoemaker-Hoard, 2005).

59 James Merrill, in an interview with John Boatwright and Enrique Ucelay DaCal, in J. D. McClatchy and Stephen Yenser, eds., *Collected Prose: James Merrill*, p. 71, 2004. Knopf.

60 Lord Moran (Charles McMoran Wilson, 1st Baron Moran of Manton), *The Anatomy of Courage*, p. 154, 2007 (1945). Constable & Robinson.

61 Oakeshott, Michael. *The Voice of Liberal Learning*, page 41 (Yale, 1989).

62 Shepherd, Reginald. *Fata Morgana,* Poems (Pittsburgh, 2007).

63 We now have another fine example of genuine birds finding their way into creative work, as queer singer/songwriter Sparkbird (Stephan Nance) managed to get Glaucous-winged Gulls into the lyrics of their song "Grey and Green," from the album *Look at the Harlequins* (2019), which took some doing.

64 Inside Higher Education - http://www.insidehighered.com/

65 Byron Herbert Reece, *Bow Down in Jericho*, 1950. 1985 printing, Cherokee, Atlanta (Marietta).

66 "Antinous" was originally written in English and is in the public domain.

67 Published as *Antinous, David & Jonathan*; Pessoa, Fernando; Reece, Byron Herbert; Alan Contreras, ed. (Oregon Review Books, 2014).

68 Edward Hirsch, *The demon and the angel* (Harcourt, 2002).

69 *The Collected Works of John Jay Chapman,* Melvin Bernstein ed. (M&S, Weston, Mass. (currently Rhode Island), 1970).

70 Patrick Sullivan is now deceased.

71 "Reflections on Poetry and Disaster," preceding pages.

72 James Merrill, in an interview with John Boatwright and Enrique Ucelay DaCal, p. 72 in J. D. McClatchy and Stephen Yenser, eds., *Collected Prose: James Merrill* (2004, Knopf).

73 Chapman, John Jay, *Practical Agitation*, 1900, revised ed. 1909, p. 49. Moffat, Yard. Reprinted in Melvin Bernstein, ed., *Collected Works of John Jay Chapman*, Vol. 2, 1970. M&S, Providence, RI.

74 Merwin,W.S. *The Lice*, 1967.

75 Merwin, W. S. *The Vixen* (Knopf, 1995).

76 Lauterbach, Ann. *The Night Sky: writings on the poetics of experience* (Viking, 2005).

77 Hemphill, Essex. *Ceremonies* (Penguin, 1992).

78 Phillips, Carl. *Coin of the Realm* (Graywolf, 2004).

79 Phillips, Carl: *In the Blood* (Northeastern, 1992), *From the Devotions* (Reginald mis-remembered the title), (Graywolf, 1998), *Riding Westwards* (FSG, 2006), *Cortege*, (Graywolf, 1995), *The Rest of Love*, (FSG, 2004).

80 See extended discussion in *Song After All.*
81 See following page.
82 Eisenberg, Evan. *The Recording Angel* (Knopf, 1988, second edition Yale, 2005), *The Ecology of Eden* (Penguin, 1998).
83 Reprinted courtesy of the author from *The Chronicle Review,* Volume 53, Issue 47, Page B5, July 27, 2007. See also his more recent *The Trumpiad* (Terra Nova, 2019). See his site: https://www.evaneisenberg.com/works.htm
84 Shetley, Vernon. *After the Death of Poetry: Poet and Audience in Contemporary America* (Duke, 1993).
85 This refers most particularly to Adam Kirsch's review of Merrill's Collected Poems ("All That Glitters," *The New Republic*, May 7, 2001) but I have heard the notion elsewhere as well. Although Merrill had no qualms about his enjoyment of bouncing words off one another, poems such as "The Country of a Thousand Years of Peace," written to honor the 26-year life of his friend the Dutch poet Hans Lodeizen, are hardly superficial and stand comparison to the work of the best poets of any age.
86 The Atkins Diet was a thing at the time this was written.
87 Craigslist has discontinued this category.
88 A Personal Digital Assistant (PDA) was a kind of precursor to a smart phone.
89 This was written before the advent of what are now called gay dating apps, e.g. Grindr, Scruff and so on.
90 Shepherd, Reginald. *Orpheus in the Bronx: Essays on Identity, Politics and the Freedom of Poetry* (Michigan, 2008).
91 Lederer, Richard. *Crazy English*, (Pocket Books, 1990).
92 Wiman, Christian. *Ambition and Survival: Becoming a Poet* (Copper Canyon, 2007).
93 Shepherd, Reginald ed. *Anthology of New American Poetries* (Iowa, 2004).
94 Ross, Alex. *The Rest is Noise: Listening to the 20th Century* (FSG, 2007).
95 Chanda, Nayan. *Bound Together: How Traders, Preachers, Adventurers, and Warriors Shaped Globalization* (Yale, 2007).
96 See "Ned Rorem and the Future of American Song," p. 105.
97 The shorter work I was thinking of is "Mountain Song," for flute and piano, performed by Fenwick Smith and Mihae Lee, Naxos.
98 Kirsch, Adam. *The Modern Element* (Norton, 2008).
99 Merrill, James. *The Changing Light at Sandover* (Atheneum, 1982).
100 Shepherd, Reginald ed. *Lyric Postmodernisms: An Anthology of Contemporary Innovative Poetries* (Counterpath, 2007).
101 Ashenburg, Katherine. *The Dirt on Clean* (North Point Press, 2007).
102 This refers to the series of "Aubrey-Maturin" novels by Patrick O'Brian, beginning with *Master and Commander*. A cookbook that attempts to replicate all of the unusual foods mentioned in the series has been published:

Anne Chotzinoff Grossman and Lisa Grossman Thomas, *Lobscouse and Spotted Dog* (Norton, 1997).

103 Hennessy, Christopher. *Outside the Lines: talking with contemporary gay poets* (Michigan, 2005).

104 "The Moated Castles of Today's Poetry," see p. 133.

105 Material from Christopher Hennessy's publication is reprinted here by gracious permission from Hennessy.

106 Delany, Samuel R. *The Jewel-Hinged Jaw*. (Dragon [hardcover], Berkley [paper], 1977).

107 Adorno, Theodor. *Aesthetic Theory*. (Routledge and Kegan Paul, 1984).

108 Adorno, Theodor. *Notes to Literature, 1991-92*. (Columbia).

109 "The Risk of Reading," not included in this reprint.

110 "Gay Male Poetry Post Identity Politics Part 2," see Shepherd's blog.

111 Muir, Edwin. *The Estate of Poetry* (Graywolf, 1962, 1993).

112 Clover, Joshua. *Madonna Anno Domini*, (Louisiana State, 1997). Louisiana State. I concur with Reginald that this book is well worth reading and is superior to *The Totality for Kids* (California, 2006). It is not easy, but it rewards revisiting, thus a poetic cognate of Stravinsky's "Rite of Spring."

113 Merrill was not the only detached poet of the era. Robert Duncan once wrote that he finally voted at age 49 because he "couldn't stand the idea of Nixon being in… I was a perfectly honest anarchist before that, never voted." See Lisa Jarnot, *Robert Duncan: The Ambassador from Venus*, p. 282 (California, 2012).

114 Stevens, Wallace. *The Collected Poems* (Knopf, 1954, Vintage, 1990).

115 Delany, Samuel R. *About Writing* (Wesleyan, 2005).

116 Le Guin, Ursula K. *The Dispossessed* (Harper, 1974).

117 Disch, Thomas M. *Camp Concentration* (Doubleday, 1969).

118 Delany, Samuel R. *Longer Views* (Wesleyan, 1996).

119 I learned one and only one thing from Ronald Reagan, the word "keister."

120 Hillman, Brenda. *Death Tractates* (Wesleyan, 1992).

121 Ashbery, John. *The Double Dream of Spring* (Dutton, 1970).

122 McDowell, Robert. *Quiet Money* (Holt, 1987).

123 Merrill, James. *Recitative* (North Point, 1986). Reprinted in J.D. McClatchy and Stephen Yenser, eds., *Collected Prose of James Merrill* (Knopf, 2004).

124 My comment on "millers" is an unattributed reference (sounds nicer than "theft") to a piece of dialogue in one of Patrick O'Brian's Aubrey-Maturin novels. I had just sent Reginald the cookbook that included recipes for all of the foods included in the novels.

125 Camus, Albert. *Notebooks 1935-1942*, p. 42 (Modern Library, 1965).

126 Parini, Jay. *Why Poetry Matters* (Yale, 2008).

127 Malheur Field Station, Harney County, Oregon.

128 The June 10-11 messages were originally received out of order but have been arranged here in proper sequence, with a couple of inquiries about the sequence deleted.

129 Kirsch, Adam. *Invasions* (Ivan R. Dee, Chicago, 2008).

About the author

Alan Contreras is a graduate of the University of Oregon and its law school. His writing has appeared in the *Stanford Law and Policy Review, Oregon English Journal, Chronicle of Higher Education, Free Inquiry, Inside Higher Education, Gay and Lesbian Review* and many other venues.

He served as co-editor of *Birds of Oregon* (Oregon State U. Press, 2003). OSU Press also published *Afield* (2009), his memoir about the experience of watching birds for 40 years, *Edge of Awe*, an edited volume of essays about the Malheur-Steens region of Oregon, and *A History of Oregon Ornithology* (2022).

Other books include *Pursuit of Happiness: The Libertarian Ethos of C.E.S. Wood* and *The Mind on Edge: An Introduction to John Jay Chapman's Philosophy of Higher Education*. He edited *TransPacific: Collected Poems of Ernest G. Moll* and co-edited the *Collected Poems of Ada Hastings Hedges*. He has also published poetry, essays and reviews in several venues. He lives in Eugene, Oregon.